Summer of '65

The Adventures and Misadventures of a Teenage World Traveler

Kent Earnest

Strategic Book Publishing and Rights Co.

Strategic Book Publishing and Rights Co.
12620 FM 1960, Suite A4-507
Houston TX 77065
www.sbpra.com

ISBN: 978-1-62516-830-6

Dedicated to my brother Gary
who died too young to see
and experience the wonders of the world
and
to my son Brett
who encouraged me to tell this story

Contents

List of Maps

Preface

This story has been nearly fifty years in the making.

In the summer of 1965, as an idealistic, short, skinny, red-headed kid, I traveled to the Holy Land and the cities of Jerusalem and Bethlehem by way of New York City, southern Europe, and the Middle East, and returned along North Africa, completely circumnavigating the Mediterranean Sea. To complete the trip, I visited Canada on the way home. The trip took eighty-seven days and was the first and longest of many trips I have taken throughout the world.

I was born in Garden City, Kansas—the county seat of Finney County situated in the southwest part of the state—and raised in the small town of Holcomb just five miles west of Garden City. In the 1950s and 1960s, Finney County was a center of both irrigated and dry-land farming, oil and gas production, and cattle feed lots. By the 1980s, the number of cattle feed lots multiplied and beef packing plants became the area's largest employer.

My father was a World War II veteran, general laborer, and postmaster, and my paternal grandfather was a tenant farmer and horse trader who occasionally boot-legged Colorado whiskey to help feed his family during the Great Depression and the lean years of the 1940s. In those two generations, travel—at least international travel—was uncommon in our family. Admittedly, in the farming area of western Kansas, none but the wealthy traveled outside the United States. There was one notable exception. My dad and three of his five brothers served in World War II, three in the Pacific theater. The oldest son in uniform landed at Omaha Beach and marched with Patton all the way into Germany. My paternal grandparents traveled throughout much of the Western US, but never ventured east of Missouri or outside the United States.

Like millions of others who served in uniform, dad scrambled to find decent work after the war. On more than one occasion, he sought work as a welder or general laborer in eastern New Mexico near Roswell, Artesia, and Carlsbad. For a few months, I went to first and second grade at Eddy Elementary School in Carlsbad where Dan Blocker taught first grade—or did until he found a better gig playing the middle son, Hoss Cartwright, on the *Bonanza* TV series. A couple of years later, I attended two months of fourth grade just outside Fort Knox, Kentucky. Two or three times dad and mom took me to Colorado Springs, Colorado and the Cheyenne Mountain Zoo. My grandparents took me to see their son in Grand Island, Nebraska, and except for an uncle taking me to see the Kansas City Athletics and New York Yankees play baseball in Kansas City a few times, that was the extent of my travels.

Few can explain why wanderlust and the urge to see the unknown is strong in some and almost non-existent in others. Perhaps the desire to travel begins at an early age. Long before I became a teenager, my parents refrained from giving me Tonka trucks or Erector sets for Christmas. Instead, they gave me a globe of the world, a sophisticated puzzle map of the United States, and miniature statues of the presidents. My parents were proud and my teachers amazed when, by the fourth grade, I could name all the presidents and their party affiliations and identify each state solely by its silhouette (Colorado and Wyoming excepted.)

Throughout my early schooling and through my first year of college, I reveled in the study of history and geography, particularly the latter. I always had an uninhibited passion for geographical discovery and a desire to see landscape, scenery, and environments I had never seen before. Growing up in the monotonous, flat farmland of western Kansas, I longed to see mountains, deserts, jungles, rivers, and oceans—and everything in between. I loved to look at maps and magazines showing pictures of other people and other countries. Like countless other young men, I especially enjoyed *National Geographic*, and not just because the magazine frequently had pictures of naked African women. Mark Twain, a noted world traveler himself, completely captured my imagination in both *The Adventures of Tom Sawyer* and *The Adventures of Huckleberry Finn.* Jack London's numerous books on his adventures in California and Alaska were equally thrilling. Even so, those stories told of domestic travels. Without question, the real gold standard for international travel was set by Marco Polo in the thirteenth century. Although his extended trip to the Orient was both ground-breaking and eye-opening, staying more than a decade in one place, seems to me, to defeat the very purpose of travel.

In addition to books, magazines, and school classes, epic movies of far-away places also impressed and inspired me during my pre-teen years, particularly two Biblical movies set in the Holy Land and Rome—*The Ten Commandments* (1956) and *Ben Hur* (1959). The miracles of Moses in his struggle with Pharaoh to free the Israelites continue to reassure the faithful. And what movie scene is more inspirational than when Ben Hur's mother and sister are cured of leprosy when the shadow of the cross passed over them? I was also inspired by two war-adventure movies—*Spartacus* (1960), also set in Rome and the Italian countryside, and *Lawrence of Arabia* (1962), set in the deserts of Jordan and Egypt. Most of the scenes from these movies were not shot on location, but I didn't know that then, and that fact didn't lessen the impression the movies made on me.

So a combination of factors, both in my early upbringing and formal education, helped develop my curiosity about the world. Hollywood's view of history, biased as it was to achieve their commercial goals, had an impact as well. Concurrently, spiritual forces intervened in my life far beyond my understanding at the time. A series of events from 1956 to 1959 overtook my psyche (if not my soul) and forever changed my perspective, not only toward international travel and satisfying my curiosity, but even on life and death itself.

In late January, 1956, my dad, a lieutenant in the Kansas Army National Guard, was scheduled for temporary training at Fort Knox. He packed mom, my six year-old brother Gary, and me in the family car, and in the middle of the night, we set off for Kentucky. We had barely traveled twelve miles when a combination of poorly marked road construction and icy conditions caused the car to overturn and Gary was killed.

The death devastated both our immediate and extended families. Dad and mom suffered the most emotionally, mentally, and psychologically, as losing a child may be the greatest burden parents can ever bear. The death seemed to hit dad the hardest because his best friend had died in an industrial accident just a year earlier.

In an effort to cope with the loss, our family turned to religion—specifically the Church of the Brethren. My parents sought spiritual comfort and guidance and I was baptized soon after. Before the accident, our family hadn't been particularly religious. The single exception was my paternal grandmother who preached infrequently as a lay minister at the local Methodist church. After the accident, our family attended church services regularly.

To deal with their loss—or to prevent me from being raised as an only child—my parents decided to have another child. In November of 1957, my second brother was born—Terry. Two years later, dad's dream finally came true when my mother gave birth to a beautiful baby girl—Cinda. But God, or Nature, or the Powers That Be were cruel once again, and the baby lived less than a month. Losing two of their four children in just over three years understandably changed my parents forever. My mother virtually withdrew from everyone except for her immediate family. When dad lost Gary, he turned to God. When he lost Cinda, he turned to whiskey. Church attendance was no longer a part of our family life and home life often became unpleasant for me.

The third event that touched not only our family but our entire community was the cold-blooded murder of four members of the most prominent family in town— that of Herb Clutter, his wife Bonnie, their daughter Nancy, and their son Kenyon. Two others daughters were grown and had moved away. The murders occurred on 15 November, 1959, in the Clutter home, just over a half-mile from our house—and just three weeks before the death of my sister.

In 1959, Holcomb was still an unincorporated town of no more than 250 people, except when school was in session and the population doubled. Like thousands of other towns in America, Holcomb and the nearby area was a community surrounded by peaceful, quiet, hard-working farm families destined to remain in the scrap-heap of history. The Clutter murders, however, forever changed the town's notoriety, most notably because Truman Capote wrote his masterpiece, *In Cold Blood*, about the murders and the two killers who committed them. Subsequently, several movies were made about the event. Afterward, Holcomb, Garden City, and *In Cold*

Blood became forever linked in history, regardless of the desires of local residents.

Capote worked on his classic throughout the early 1960s and the book was published in 1966, a few months after I returned from my trip. As postmaster of Holcomb (appointed by President John Kennedy in 1962), dad took great pride in frequently being Capote's point of contact while he was doing his on-site research. Grandpa added to his stable of horses when he bought Nancy Clutter's gentle mare "Babe." My young brother and the kids from the entire neighborhood rode Babe, and grandpa always enjoyed showing off the horse to newspaper and magazine reporters who covered the Clutter story for years afterward.

The killers were caught in Las Vegas, Nevada, tried and convicted in Garden City, and executed at the Kansas State Penitentiary in Lansing, Kansas in April 1965, just six weeks before my trip began. Capote witnessed the hangings, the last men in Kansas to be executed in that manner.

These three circumstances—two sibling deaths and the predictable family strife that followed, along with a notoriously brutal family murder—had a profound impact on me. As an eighteen-year-old in 1965, I was looking for a trip that satisfied my temporal curiosity and at the same time allowed me to seek spiritual awareness. Coupled with my earthly desire to see foreign lands, what better place to seek an epiphany or to find answers to life's questions than the places where Jesus once walked? Somewhere along the line—no specific date stands out—I chose to go to the Holy Land.

Getting there, however, posed a real problem. I had no detailed plan, little money, and my parents could offer nothing but moral support. I thought perhaps I could just walk and catch a few rides along the way.

Introduction

The years from 1954 to 1974 were possibly the most volatile twenty-year period in our nation's history. One could argue the cultural, racial, political, and military upheaval during this time may have affected the daily lives of far more US citizens than the Civil War had a century earlier or World War II had a half generation before.

Brown vs. the Topeka Board of Education (1954) ruled integration in public schools would be the law of the land. Governor Orval Faubus of Arkansas ignored the law (1957) and dared someone to enforce it in Little Rock. President Dwight Eisenhower did just that. Five years later, James Meredith became the first black student to attend the University of Mississippi. That same year, the United States and the Soviet Union narrowly avoided nuclear holocaust, but the US became more involved in a land war in Asia. Despite being popular, President John Kennedy was assassinated in November 1963. In 1965, President Johnson signed the Civil Rights Act, which among other things, allowed black Americans to vote for the first time (in real numbers) since Reconstruction waned in the 1880s. That same year, Johnson signed Medicare and Medicaid into law. Race riots and civil unrest occurred in Los Angeles, Detroit, and several southern cities despite the pleas for passive disobedience from America's greatest civil rights leader, Reverend Martin Luther King, Jr. King was assassinated in April 1968 and only two months later, while running for President, Robert Kennedy was also assassinated. Marches against the war were commonplace. In 1968, Richard Nixon won the Presidency partly based on a "secret" plan to end the war in Vietnam. Nixon's plan didn't end the war and in 1970, the Ohio National Guard killed four peaceful war protesters at Kent State University and wounded nearly a dozen others. Nixon won re-election in 1972, resigned in disgrace two years later, and the war in Vietnam continued. The war would not end until April, 1975 at a cost of more than 58,000 US lives. Aside from these events, things were quiet in America in my late teens and early twenties.

Without question, the war in Vietnam dominated the thoughts of most draft-eligible young men in America in the 1960s, including me. Dutifully, I signed up for the Selective Service when I turned eighteen, just as the law required. I had no choice really; dad was a patriot's patriot and I could have more easily swum the Atlantic Ocean than avoid being in uniform while a war was going on. With Vietnam in the back of my mind, I decided if I was going on a trip, I'd better leave soon.

In the middle of this political and racial upheaval and continued unrest that defined the 1960s, and before Vietnam descended into the escalating quagmire it would become, I decided to take my trip of discovery. The trip was not a crusade. I wasn't trying to liberate the Holy Land from the Muslims or anybody else for that matter. King Richard the Lion-Hearted and other European monarchs tried that a millennium ago with limited success. No, my trip was more like that of Captains Lewis and Clark who sought a northwest passage in America nearly two centuries before. Admittedly, I wasn't looking for a new shipping route, but I might discover a little about the world, a little about the Holy Land, and just perhaps a whole lot about myself. I would leave the racial unrest and America's other domestic problems in the capable hands of President Johnson and his rubber-stamp Congress and set out on my own trip of discovery.

I say "trip." I never say "vacation" because although my trip was an intellectual adventure, it was not a vacation. Vacations often consist of visiting national parks, theme parks, or beach resorts, or attending concerts, sporting events, or taking cruises. When people are on vacation, someone makes their bed every day and sometimes they even have breakfast in bed (unless they're camping.) They eat at nice restaurants and kids get to stay up as late at night as they want. Most notably, when people go on vacation, they're almost always with friends or family.

Not me. This was not a vacation, I was not with friends or family, and I most assuredly did not enjoy luxuries. From my perspective, the top of the vacation luxury list included hotel beds, showers, and good meals. Many nights I did without either a bed or a shower and often ate only bread or crackers. No, this was not a vacation; it was simply an alluring trip of discovery—nothing more, nothing less.

Both the plan and the money to take me halfway around the world and back were nebulous. The plan to get there, one might say, was ill-conceived. I knew the Holy Land was at the east end of the Mediterranean Sea, a couple of continents and an ocean away, but that's about all the detail I needed at the time. After all, I'd always had a good sense of direction; what else could I possibly need?

Money was the real issue. (Isn't it always?) I could expect no help from my parents, so in the fall of 1964, I diligently took on three jobs while maintaining my full-time status as a freshman at Garden City Junior College. I was unable to work in the spring of 1965 since I was passionately involved as a distance runner for the college track team and there was little time to do anything but train and compete. When the time came to begin the trip, I had saved exactly $750.

In 1965, $750 was not a lot of money, but if you tripled or quadrupled that amount, you could buy a brand-new car. That amount certainly wasn't enough to travel first class from Kansas to the Holy Land and back. More accurately, the money I saved allowed me to travel only on a shoe-string budget. I would have to scrimp and save and deny myself standard travel amenities like quality food, hotel rooms, souvenirs, and expensive transportation. To accomplish this never-to-be-forgotten jaunt, I would be forced to spend as little as possible getting myself from one place to another. Hitchhiking seemed the most viable option.

* * *

Scores of books have been written about hitchhiking, a number of them pontificate about the magic, romantic, almost karmic impression one feels walking in the great outdoors. Some say that the path to enlightenment begins by standing on a roadside with your thumb out ready to catch a ride and a conversation with a perfect stranger. Horse manure! There may be something self-satisfying about walking along a winding mountain road on a sunny, 65° day in the beautiful Pacific Northwest. It's quite another thing, however, to wait hours for a ride at an isolated intersection in the Sahara Desert when the temperature is 115° in the shade and you're out of water. To me, hitchhiking was and remains simply an inexpensive method of getting from one location to another. If you have a chance to take a bus, train, or boat, by all means take them. I did. During my trip, I rode in cars, trucks, and buses; trains and subways; boats, ships, ferries, and gondolas; and motor scooters, farm combines, donkey carts, and a camel!

Let me provide a cursory overview about hitchhiking. Properly preparing to hitchhike involves bringing a tent, sleeping bag, rain coat, flashlight, map, magic marker (to make signs indicating where you want to go), camera, the ubiquitous backpack, and most essentially, toilet paper. (Just as a child will put his finger in an electric socket only once, a hitchhiker will forget toilet paper only one time.) Knowing the national language and the local hitchhiking laws is beneficial as well.

In the summer of '65, I was armed with none of that—except the TP. As the only hitchhiker I ever saw without a backpack, I put a few changes of clothes in a faded gold 1940s hardback suitcase borrowed from my grandmother. The suitcase held far fewer clothes than the standard backpack, but it had a distinct advantage—I could set the suitcase on end and use it as a seat, which was particularly useful during long waits between rides. I never had a map until I found one at the site of a car wreck in Algeria after eighty-five percent of my trip was complete.

Before I put the issue to rest, some important points about hitchhiking must be made. First, the three most important factors in getting a ride are: location, location, location. Ideally, there needs to be some traffic, but not too much. Drivers must be able to see hitchhikers early, and the location must be in a place where the driver can pull over safely. (It also doesn't hurt if the hitchhiker looks clean-cut and non-threatening.) On my trip to the Holy Land and back, I followed the "location" tenant of hitchhiking consistently.

Second, some books on hitchhiking say to be prepared to walk all day. Not me. As a competitive runner in high school and college and as a marathon runner, I have never cared for walking much. I can truthfully say that during my trip of nearly 20,000 miles, I walked fewer than ten—perhaps fewer than five. That figure, of course, is mileage outside city limits. I walked many miles inside cities, particularly when seeking tourist attractions or getting to the edge of the city to catch a ride to the next town. In big cities particularly, I always took a bus or taxi to just outside of town—if I had the money.

Once I caught a ride, I never asked to get out of the car due to anxiety or feeling uncomfortable or unsafe with the driver. Admittedly, speeding drivers, (and there were many in Italy) scared the hell out of me. Between fast drivers and my refusal to stop in late afternoon or early evening to look for a hotel, I covered the miles much faster than other hitchhikers. I tried to limit my hitchhiking to daylight hours. To do otherwise would defeat a primary purpose of travel—to see the country. But frequently, I got caught outside of cities or towns at sundown and I couldn't rent a hotel room even if I had had plenty of money, which I didn't.

A final, critical point about hitchhiking is this: a world of difference exists between hitchhiking in America and hitchhiking in foreign countries. To begin with, some foreign travel requires specific inoculations before you leave the US. And unlike crossing state borders in the US, crossing national borders nearly always requires a passport and clearance through both customs and immigration. Additionally, many countries require a visa—an added layer of bureaucracy and expense. Getting to know the country's cultural customs and exchanging money is often a hassle. International hitch-hikers face a constant challenge knowing whether or not to exchange money at their hotel, at a bank, or through the black market on the street.

Conversely, hitchhikers and drivers in America use the same money and read the same maps and road signs. Most significantly, in America, drivers and hitchhikers speak the same language. In many foreign countries, hitchhikers and drivers do not speak the same language. This one issue—the simple lack of communication—causes more trouble than anything else during international hitchhiking.

I took my trip long before the advent and common usage of cell phones or the Internet and I only called home one time from outside the United States—at the end of my trip. But, I wrote dozens of letters. I had a young girlfriend, Loretta, still in high school. Our relationship would not develop seriously until I returned from my trip and during my first two years in the Army. Still, I was closer to her than anyone but my parents, so I kept the three of them informed of where I was, how I was doing, and what significant things I saw. Admittedly, by the time they got my letters, I was long gone from the places where I mailed them.

I have been asked many times why I took on this adventure alone. Going alone was not my intention. My high school class and both of the classes at the junior college were small. Still, I asked scores of people—both men and women—to go with me. Most could not go even if they had wanted to, particularly the young men. In 1965, the community around Holcomb was made up mostly of strong German-Catholic farm families. I say "strong" both in their spiritual devotedness to Catholicism, and in a physical sense for the sons since they spent hours and days setting irrigation tubes for alfalfa and sugar beets, baling hay, or milking cows. Most relevantly, however, farmers' sons drove tractors, grain trucks, and combines, especially during June at the height of wheat harvest. In those days, farm labor was cheap, but family labor was free. No self-respecting wheat farmer with an eye on his pocketbook would allow a son to take off during harvest time, even if someone else paid for the trip. So that was that and going alone was my only option.

Going alone wasn't all bad. I am an independent person and to have the freedom to go any direction, travel any length of time, and to stay in one place or another without having to consult another person was satisfying. Besides, with the single-minded purpose of getting to the Holy Land, I could get there far more quickly alone than if I had been with others who wished to spend more time elsewhere. I knew then as I know now, one can spend an entire summer in the culturally and historically rich cities of London, Paris, Rome, Athens, or Cairo and still not see everything. With the exception of Bethlehem and Jerusalem (and to a lesser extent New York City), this book addresses little about the historic and cultural attractions in the major cities I visited. On this trip, those cities just happened to be intervening stopping points on the way toward a much larger goal.

Another important point needs to be made: thousands

of hitchhikers crisscrossed Europe in the 1960s and 1970s. In 1965, the world was safe enough for nearly anyone to travel to the Middle East and North Africa using the same route and visit the same places I did. But they didn't. Or if they did, they didn't travel alone and they certainly didn't write about it. Today, much of the Arab world is in flames, particularly Syria, Palestine, Egypt, and Libya. It's not likely many hitchhikers will enter those countries in the immediate future. With the continuing unrest in the Middle East region, a generation or more might pass before first-hand travel accounts are written about these places.

* * *

Most avid readers think they can write a book. I am no different. But I did not want to write *a* book, I wanted to write *this* book. I don't know who had the idea—a family member, a teacher, a friend, or possibly I thought of it myself—but I wrote and kept a diary. The diary, several letters home, and my memory of past events, some of which are as clear in my mind as yesterday, constitute the basis for the chronology that follows. As short-story writer and Pulitzer Prize winning author Eudora Welty noted, "Whatever our theme in writing, it is old and tried. Whatever our place, it has been visited by the stranger; it will never be new again. It is only the vision that can be new; but that is enough." I do not purport my travels were new. Nor do I imply that others might not follow in my footsteps. But my "vision" and perspective as an idealistic eighteen year-old traveler nearly a half century ago is unique. I hope that is enough.

Some have asked why I took this long to tell my story. The answer is simple—life got in the way. School, a crazy Asian war, family, marriages and businesses—some successful, some not—and numerous mediocre jobs for little pay. As they say, it's always something. I'm retired now, and, simply put, I have the time.

Author Patricia Schultz noted in her *1,000 Places to See Before You Die*, "Some road warriors can speed from New York to L.A. without registering a thing: I can walk around my mid-Manhattan block and come home with a carton of milk and stories to tell." My trip as a teenager to nineteen countries was a thousand times longer than the distance around a mid-Manhattan block. And although publication itself is no proof of merit, the narrative that follows involves good, old-fashioned story telling— stories of people, places, sights, sounds, smells, and always of innumerable surprises. As I was to find out, travel can be highly exhilarating, yet unexpected situations can cause incalculable emotional turmoil.

So, in 1965 I hitchhiked to the Holy Land. But this book is not about hitchhiking as much as it is about the people, places, and events that touched my life that summer. This book is about my experiences and the broad range of raw emotions I felt when I encountered the unexpected. Love, anger, fear, happiness, sadness, joy, frustration, disappointment, disgust, sympathy, and empathy: I experienced all of these emotions and more in three short months. What does not come directly from the diary comes from my memory blemished by time and flawed by my lack of total recall. But most notably, this book is a memoir—a window into three months of my life—and perhaps into my very soul.

Leaving Kansas

Assuredly, the world was a safer place in 1965 than it is now, but I always wondered why my parents, after losing two of their four children, didn't vociferously protest my hitchhiking alone across the world at such a young age. Perhaps they thought (and rightfully so) that I would be just as safe on the streets of Rome, Damascus, Cairo, or Benghazi as the Clutter children were when they were safely tucked in their own beds on a raw, windy November night six years earlier.

Without either of my parents voicing undue anxiety or apprehension, I prepared to leave just as soon as possible after the spring semester ended in junior college. The first opportunity came on Friday, the 28th of May. Outside of some isolated storm days, I cannot recall the weather on any specific day anytime during my lifetime— with one exception. The day I left home and was truly on my own for the first time stands out as clearly in my mind today as if it were yesterday. The day was a typically warm late May afternoon and early evening in Western Kansas; the sky was beautifully blue and partially filled with puffy, cumulous clouds moving from the southwest toward the northeast.

Without misgivings, forebodings, undue apprehension, or even faint memories of a disastrous trip almost a decade earlier, I hugged and kissed my parents good-bye. We didn't know when (or if) we would see each other again. Although the ultimate goal was Bethlehem, I was unsure if I would continue east and go fully around the world, or retrace my steps through Europe or Africa. I knew the spring semester at college began sometime in January and I wanted to return in time to earn my track scholarship. Since the college had no cross-country team (traditionally a fall sport) I could accept missing the fall semester.

Perhaps a college freshman from New York, L.A., or Miami might slip off for a world trip with few people knowing about it, but not so in Holcomb. As people from a small town know well, everyone knows everyone else's business. Leaving on a trip of this magnitude was a big deal and most in Holcomb (and several in Garden City) knew about it, so finding a friend or family member to get me started in the right direction was no challenge. Bernie McPherson and his wife, friends of my dad, were going to Kansas City, so I caught a ride with them. We left at 6:25 p.m.

One of my favorite aunts lived in Kansas City, Missouri —Aunt Billie, and the ride of nearly 400 miles to her house where I spent the night was close to the longest single ride on my entire trip. However, that was not hitchhiking; it was simply catching a ride. The hitchhiking would start the following day.

Just after mid-day on Saturday, Aunt Billie's husband Bud took me east of downtown Kansas City and left me at an east-bound on-ramp on I-70. From that spot and from that time I was truly on my own and all decisions—good, bad, or indifferent—would be undeniably mine alone. After eighteen years of near-total dependence on family, I was intoxicated with the idea of freedom to make choices unencumbered by the influence of parents or others!

Within five minutes of standing at the on-ramp, a young African-American college student in a red, chrome-covered Chevy convertible offered me a ride. I jumped in immediately, saying to myself, "Hey, this hitchhiking stuff is really going to be easy." We exchanged idle chit-chat for a few miles and then he asked me if I wanted drugs. He didn't specify what drugs he was offering (or selling), but I responded by telling him I was a college runner and I didn't do drugs or alcohol, not even beer. This young man gave me my first real hitchhiking ride and was the first to offer me drugs. He would not be the last on either score. He let me off in Columbia, Missouri.

Five or six short rides later, I crossed the Mississippi River at St. Louis into Illinois when a wealthy, educated, New York City businessman—Sam Taylor—offered me a ride. He said he was going to New York City, but his mom lived in Columbus, Ohio and he had to stop and visit her for a day or two before going on. However, he offered me a ride all the way to Columbus if I wanted. I agreed. We stopped in Effingham, Illinois for the night. Sam paid for my motel room and for breakfast the next morning and at 9:30 a.m., we were off for Columbus. We had a number of lengthy conversations about a variety of topics, but one clearly stands out. He knew several strippers in New York and other ladies of easy virtue and even some young boys if I was interested. I told him I was curious about the women, but not remotely interested in the other. He gave me his business card with both his phone number and address, and I promised to call him when I got to New York. He left me off in downtown Columbus, near his mother's house.

With less than two full days of hitchhiking behind me, I had been offered drugs and sex with strangers. I thought to myself this trip might turn out to be far more unusual than I had ever imagined.

As I alluded to in the *Introduction,* the real curse of hitchhiking is being left in the middle of a big city. Hitch-hikers new to the city don't know which bus to take to the edge of the city limits or which of several highways lead into and out of town. It's easy to get the wrong road. In Columbus, I got the wrong road. I meant to take I-70 eastward toward Pennsylvania, Philadelphia specifically, and on to New York. By mistake, I got on I-71 heading northeast toward Cleveland, Ohio. A man took me as far as Akron, Ohio, where he dropped me off near the Ohio Turnpike going east into Pennsylvania. I was overjoyed when two girls quickly picked me up, but unfortunately, they got off the turnpike in only fifteen minutes. (The next time I caught a ride with two women proved to be far more eventful.)

It was about 10:00 p.m., completely dark, and after

spending well over an hour trying to catch a ride onto the turnpike, I gave up. I walked a short way to a two-lane highway and soon, a semi-truck driver picked me up. He was heading for Philadelphia. Whether he was avoiding the turnpike because of the cost or because his load was overweight (I suspect the latter), we hurtled up and down the hills of eastern Ohio and western Pennsylvania, driving far too fast to stop within the safety of the headlights. Thankfully, the driver allowed me to crawl back into his sleeper, and I was able to sleep for nearly four hours, until 3:00 a.m. or so. He stopped in Kittanning, Pennsylvania, forty-odd miles northeast of Pittsburgh and bounced my butt out of the sleeper so he could rest. He told me I was welcome to wait and we'd continue the trip once he woke up. That offer sounded like a good idea to me, so I went inside the truck stop and struck up a conversation with the all-night attendant.

When I stepped out of the truck, the unique smell of hard-rock coal—an odor often described as similar to rotten eggs—hit me full force. It was the first time I smelled hard-rock coal. Due to its high sulfur content, the smell of coal mined in Ohio, West Virginia, Pennsylvania, and eastern Kentucky is far more distinctive and pungent than the soft coal mined in Wyoming. My olfactory nerves adjusted quickly and I got used to the smell, just as western Kansans get used to the smell of cattle feedlots and beef packing plants.

The attendant told me a wage of $230 a month was good for that area and he and his wife rented a five-room

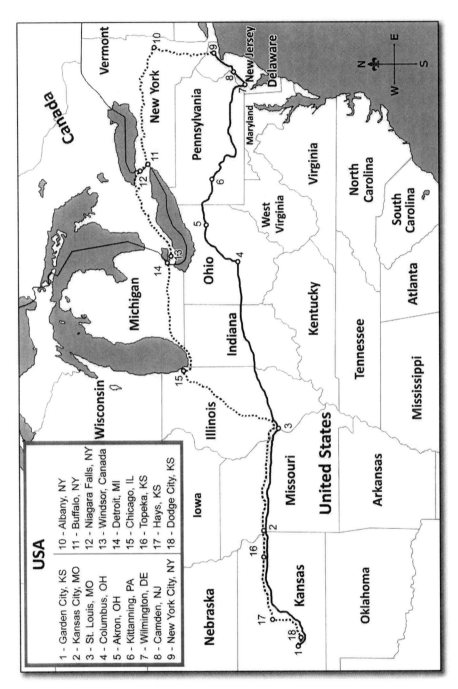

USA

1 - Garden City, KS
2 - Kansas City, MO
3 - St. Louis, MO
4 - Columbus, OH
5 - Akron, OH
6 - Kittanning, PA
7 - Wilmington, DE
8 - Camden, NJ
9 - New York City, NY
10 - Albany, NY
11 - Buffalo, NY
12 - Niagara Falls, NY
13 - Windsor, Canada
14 - Detroit, MI
15 - Chicago, IL
16 - Topeka, KS
17 - Hays, KS
18 - Dodge City, KS

Holcomb, KS to New York City, NY and Return

house in the country for $18 a month. By comparison, back home I was making more than $200 a month just from my night-clerk job at a local motel. Working from 11:00 p.m. to 7:00 a.m. seven days a week, I was clearing ninety cents an hour after taxes! Hell, I might move to Kittanning, find a coal miner's daughter, raise a passel of rug rats, and live like a king— particularly if I had two or three jobs going at once. The attendant assured me, however, that wages were much lower in western Pennsylvania than in western Kansas and the only good money in Kittanning was working in the coal mines. Unbeknownst to me at the time, 274 men lost their lives in a mining accident in Dhanbad, India the day before, and three days later, 237 perished in a coal mine explosion in Fukuoka, Japan. No, I didn't want to spend my life, or even an hour, working in a coal mine. Surely, hitchhiking or being a soldier was safer than being a coal miner.

The truck driver had told me to wake him up at 5:00 a.m. and I did, but he wanted to sleep some more. Finally, when he wasn't up by 7:00 a.m., I started hitchhiking eastward on the most curving and hilly roads in the Alleghenies. I picked up short rides until I hit Bedford, Pennsylvania, where I tried to make better time by getting on the Pennsylvania Turnpike. The problem was, all the cars were going west instead of east. No problem. I back-tracked west (not the last time I would try that maneuver) until I came to a rest stop and asked the driver to let me out. I crossed a pedestrian bridge over the turnpike to the eastbound lane, and a man and his wife took me all the way to Wilmington, Delaware.

Wilmington was too far south, of course, so after walking across the Memorial Bridge over the Delaware River and into New Jersey, I caught a couple of rides to Camden. I coaxed the last driver to take me directly to the bus station in Camden, where I bought a ticket to New York City.

New York City

Just after 1:30 a.m., I stepped out of the bus station onto the streets of New York City. I wasn't scared—I was absolutely petrified! I couldn't catch my breath, my heart raced a hundred beats a minute, and I froze in place for five or six seconds. Bright lights and people were everywhere and I couldn't see the tops of the buildings! Cautiously and deliberately, I sidestepped ten or fifteen feet to my right, carefully feeling the wall behind me. I was certain at any second now someone would club me or rob me and take everything I had. Well, they weren't going to attack me from behind because my back and butt were firmly pasted to the building's bricks. I released my white-knuckled grip from the suitcase handle and slid the suitcase between my legs. Slowly, my breathing returned to normal and my heart quit pounding. I stopped there a few minutes to regain my composure and to survey the situation.

I was on 42nd Street, it was damn near 2:00 a.m., and there were people everywhere. I saw perhaps 80 or 100 or 120 people. What in the hell were that many people doing out at that time of night? Many were walking, some were standing on street corners, a few were sitting in the doorways of closed businesses, and two or three were either sleeping, drunk, or both, right on the sidewalk. City folks joke about small-town America folding up the sidewalks at five or six in the evening, but the stereotype is true. I was seeing more people at 2:00 a.m. in New York City than I had ever seen on Main Street in Garden City, even during the height of the Christmas shopping season.

About fifteen or twenty yards to my right was an intersection with traffic lights. I watched the lights change twelve or fifteen times while I contemplated my next move. On the other side of the street, about halfway down the block, I saw a hotel. With great trepidation I decided to go for it. Tightly clutching my suitcase, I walked briskly with the traffic lights. Carefully and quite noticeably, I'm sure, I turned around every five or six steps to see if anyone was sneaking up on me. After what felt like ten minutes but was probably no more than a minute or so, I reached the sanctuary—I mean hotel lobby.

Unfortunately, the hotel, at $10 to $15 a night, was way beyond my means, so I asked the clerk for a recommendation for a less expensive hotel and went back out on the streets. I checked three or four other hotels before settling on Hotel Strand, just off 42nd Street. A bargain, if you can call a dump a bargain at $5.25 a night. The first room the bellhop showed me was so narrow I could only get into the bed from the end—not from either side. I demanded better. I settled on a room just wide enough for one person to stand on each side of the bed. What an upgrade! Except for a few shaky hours of sleep in the truck's sleeper outside of Kittanning, I hadn't slept for two days.

I slept more soundly than if I was in the finest room in the Waldorf Astoria. I didn't awake until 1:30 in the afternoon. If a maid knocked on the door to clean the room or make the bed, I didn't hear her. As soon as I got up, I went straight to the window to see the wonderful view of New York City—in the daytime. When I pulled up the shade, I saw I was twenty stories high and facing a solid brick wall only twelve inches away. A sliver of early afternoon sunlight filtered down the chasm between the two buildings. I thought if a fat person wanted to jump to his or her death, they would be unable to do so from this place; they'd get stuck before they got halfway to the ground. I vowed to myself then and there to always ask for a hotel room with a view.

I checked out of the Strand and with suitcase in hand, wandered around for an hour or two looking for a better hotel. I finally chose the Tudor Hotel, located close to 42nd Street. I paid an exorbitant $8.40 a night, but at least I had a window looking down on the busy streets below.

New York City has been the most populous city in America since the first census was taken in 1790. But the city is more than just a population center; it's a cultural crossroads with over 800 languages spoken. In addition, the city is a major center for entertainment and the performing arts, home to multiple sports franchises in football, basketball, and baseball, and the economic center of the world. The land and water area encompasses nearly 500 square miles, yet the city is easy to get around. The subway system, one of the most extensive in the world, covers more than 700 miles. Transportation is complemented by thousands of buses and millions of cabs—well, perhaps not quite that many.

Admittedly, a person can do a thousand different things in New York City—more than one person can do in a week, a month, or an entire summer for that matter. I knew little of arts or culture, less about science, and nothing about economics. I focused on what I did know—baseball—and finding an affordable way to get to Europe.

After four days, my suitcase felt like an appendage to my body, so when I left it at the hotel, I became free as a bird to move about the city. I didn't fly, but I took my first subway ride and headed straight for the New York World's Fair in Flushing Meadows, in the borough of Queens. The fair's theme was "Peace through Understanding," symbolized by a giant, twelve-story-high, stainless-steel globe—a truly impressive sight. I got a great deal more enjoyment, however, going to the Wax Museum where life-like imitations of famous people, both living and dead, appeared uncannily realistic. Without enthusiasm, I rode a couple of carnival rides and found they're far less enjoyable when a person is alone. I saw Shea Stadium from a distance, but it was dark because the Mets were out of town.

I returned to the hotel a little after 10:00 p.m. but

quickly went outside to walk the nearby streets—42nd Street, Broadway, and down to Times Square—the brightly illuminated hub of the Broadway theatre district. Times Square is purported to be the busiest pedestrian intersection in the world and I went there just to satisfy my curiosity and watch the people. That's why most tourists go to Times Square; to watch the people and see the neon signs flash the latest world news and advertise the world's latest fashions. Within less than a day in New York City, I had ridden a subway, attended the World's Fair, and then walked the streets at night as calmly as if I had lived there all my life. What a colossal change in attitude and perspective from a mere twenty-four hours earlier when I had first stepped outside that bus station!

Getting from Holcomb to New York by land had been relatively easy, particularly with the great jump start to Kansas City and the three-state sojourn through Illinois, Indiana, and half of Ohio with Sam Taylor. Getting across the Atlantic Ocean, however, was another matter. Earlier, dad and I thought I might hire on as a deck hand on a commercial freighter and earn my way across the seas. I was about to find out.

Before 8:00 a.m. the next day, I headed for the piers, but all I saw was passenger ships. A couple of the passenger ship fares were affordable, around $250, but the ships didn't leave for several days. A ship was leaving for Dakar, Senegal the next day, but the fare was $375, a full half of my starting funds. If I went that far south, I might have a hell of a time navigating up the west coast of Africa to Morocco and eastward across North Africa. I decided to pass on Dakar.

A tip led me to the Seafarer's Union building where some union members bounced me out on the street because I was not a union member. A Swedish sailor there told me to go to 62 Hanson Place to meet a ship's captain bound for Norway and Sweden. The sailor was unsure of when the ship was leaving, but he assured me if a full crew had not been hired, I could sign on as a non-union member. Still, Norway and Sweden seemed too far north, as I was inclined to take a more direct route. As I left the Union building, another sailor offered to take me in his car to meet a couple of ship captains to see if anything might be worked out. As it turned out, the sailor was gay (although we used another word in those days) and he had ulterior motives for me. I jumped out of the car as quickly as possible and hurried back to the hotel, getting there about 5:30 p.m.

After a refreshing shower, I took the subway to Yankee Stadium, but the game was rained out so I back-tracked to Coney Island. On the way back to the hotel, I went to the top of the Empire State Building, the tallest building in the world from 1931 to 1972. The day was not a total loss and I especially enjoyed the last three or four hours. Coney Island and its carnival atmosphere coupled with standing at the top of the Empire State Building overlooking New York City at night remains a cherished memory. Nonetheless, I wasn't any closer to getting to Europe.

The next day, the hotel bellhop advised me to find ship departures in the daily paper. He also advised me to visit the main offices of various shipping lines, since most had ships going to different places around the world. I took his advice and soon found myself in the main offices of the United States Lines where I was presented with a number of options. The best fare available was $180 to England, but that ship wouldn't leave until June 9th— another six days. Another one of their ships left for England the next day, but I needed a yellow fever shot to board passage. To this day, I have no idea why a yellow fever shot was required for passage to Europe. The jungles of Africa, South America, or Asia I understood. But a yellow fever shot for travel to Europe simply didn't make sense. Nonetheless, I couldn't get to Europe without the shot. I was advised the best place to get it was at Idlewild Airport. Three hours later, I made it to Idlewild and they administered the shot for free. Excitedly, I returned to my hotel to call my folks and tell them about my passage to England. I was disappointed, though, to come all the way to New York and fail to see a Yankees' game.

The next morning, I rushed to the United States Lines to pay for passage to England. The ship was the *SS Pioneer Tide,* not a passenger ship per se, but a freighter carrying cars and other dry goods to England's busiest seaport in Southampton. The fare was $232, a goodly portion of the funds I had, but there was a real advantage. I was getting a "lift" of some 3,000 miles, plus three meals a day and a bed for eight or ten nights or however long it took to cross the Atlantic. I couldn't wait to leave, but before I dashed back to the hotel to pick up my suitcase, the clerk told me the ship's departure was delayed for three days. The *Tide* was now scheduled for a 7:00 a.m. departure on Monday, June 7th.

That was good news and bad news. Naturally, I was anxious to get on my way again, but at the same time, I had a full weekend to spend in New York—and the Yankees were in town! Not only that, once I paid for my passage, I would be able to eat and sleep on the ship until it departed, as everything was included in the fare. I got my suitcase from the hotel, stowed it away on the *Tide,* and briefly said hello to a young British man who apparently was also going to be a passenger. By then it was 4:00 p.m. and I excitedly dashed off to Yankee Stadium for a night game.

I always loved baseball and had been good—defensively—even at a young age. At a Pittsburgh Pirates' tryout camp two years earlier, I was the only infielder to never miss a ball or throw badly to first base. The coaching staff took several notes on my play and I was euphoric that the dream was alive. At a second camp the following year, they made me run thirty-yard sprints. I was a distance runner—not a sprinter—so I failed miserably. They had me bat, too, and I couldn't hit what I couldn't see. My dream of playing professional baseball died that day, but the love of the game stayed with me for a lifetime. In fact, in 1979, I named my only son Brett after George Brett, the sole Kansas City Royal in baseball's Hall of Fame.

To play in Yankee Stadium—the House That Ruth Built—is the pinnacle of baseball stadiums for almost every major league ball player. To a baseball fan, Yankee Stadium is as inspiring and magical as the Vatican is to Catholics, Mecca is to the Islamic faithful, or Mt. Everest is to mountain climbers. To real baseball fanatics, sitting in Yankee Stadium for the first time and to soak up the history, nostalgia, and ambiance is truly one of life's most cherished memories. Certainly it was for me. The game I saw that night was remarkable; no score for either side through fourteen innings. The Chicago White Sox won the game with two runs in the top of the fifteenth.

The extra-inning game made it very late when I returned to the ship, so I slept until 11:30 the next morning. I got up just in time to have the noon meal on the *Tide.* For an hour or so, I chatted with a fifty-year-old German crew member about the many places he had seen in the world. I thought that provided a person didn't mind staying single, a seaman's life might be a fascinating one. The lifestyle of a sailor seemed far more exciting and certainly much safer than working in a coal mine.

My conversation with the sailor made me late getting to the afternoon game at Yankee Stadium. For the second day in a row, the game went into extra innings, with the Yankees winning 4-3 in ten innings. After the Yankees' game, I noticed a pick-up game between some teenagers at Babe Ruth Field only two or three blocks from the Stadium, so I joined in and played until dark. Too early to return to the boat, I caught the subway for a second trip to Coney Island and returned to the *Tide* a little after midnight.

Just like the day before, I slept late, getting up just in time for dinner. Once again, I hurried to the ballpark. I returned to the *Tide* immediately after the game and spent the rest of the evening reading. In the ship's galley, I met the night steward who stirred my imagination with his tales of world travel. As a merchant marine sailor, he had been to all the continents except Antarctica. He had also done some acting and producing (he didn't say what movie) and he was doing some writing along with his duties as a ship's officer. We must have visited for well over three hours and when I went to bed, it was almost 3:00 a.m.

The ship's scheduled departure at 7:00 a.m. on Monday, June 7th slipped back to 10:00 a.m. I was so overwhelmed with the disembarking process that I slept right through it. No matter. We weren't going far just yet. We stopped to take on more cargo at Brooklyn Army Base a short distance away. I got off the ship in the afternoon and walked the streets of Brooklyn for a couple of hours, returning in time for the evening meal. I read a little more, and then watched the sun go down over New York while waiting for the ship to sail.

It took just over twelve hours to get everything loaded at Brooklyn Army Base. At 10:45 p.m. we finally got underway. Looking at the city at night from New York Harbor as the ship slowly made its way toward the Atlantic was a sight like no other. That night, the Empire

State Building dominated the skyline as it would for another five years before the twin towers of the World Trade Center were completed. A billion lights transformed the city's nightscape into a dazzling spectacle unlike any other in the world, except perhaps for Hong Kong. As the city lights faded and the darkness of the open sea enveloped the ship, I realized I was so wrapped up in the excitement of New York—the ballgames, arranging for passage to Europe, and riding the subway for hours just for fun—that I had forgotten to call Sam Taylor. I never did call him.

I spent a full seven days in New York City— more time than I would spend in other city on my trip, with the exception of Bethlehem. Only one short week in New York, but I felt so much older and wiser. Now, I had been somewhere and I'd seen some things. Not places the sailors on the *Tide* had seen, but I was on my way.

The Crossing

Headquartered in New York City, the United States Lines was a transatlantic shipping company founded in 1921 by "stealing" two of their first three ships from the Germans. Exhibiting the full power of both nepotism and political cronyism, President Teddy Roosevelt's son Kermit was one of the company's founding owners when two German-made cargo ships were seized during World War I and kept as reparations. The company grew and twenty years later, many of the vessels were used during World War II as troop ships to transport soldiers and sailors to Europe and back.

The flagship of the United States Lines—the *SS United States*—was built in 1952 with the help of an enormous federal subsidy and was the largest and fastest passenger ship ever constructed in the US. (It remains so to this day.) The ship operated until 1969 when competition from airlines brought the glory days of passenger service to an end.

In 1965 the company still had more than three dozen cargo ships, one of which was the *SS Pioneer Tide*. The ship was built in California and launched in 1945. She was 435 feet long, 63 feet wide, and weighed 8,276 gross tons. Originally named the *SS Spitfire,* the ship was purchased in 1948 by the United States Lines and renamed the *SS Pioneer Tide.* The ship was sold in 1969 and two more times after that, changing its name each time. Designed primarily to haul cars, metal shipping containers, and various dry goods, the *Tide* was also outfitted to carry passengers and a crew of fewer than forty. Depending upon weather conditions, the *Tide* might cross the Atlantic in eight days, about two days longer than the luxurious *SS United States.* (I found out later that in May 1975, the *Tide* ran aground on a beach near Karachi, Pakistan and was scrapped.)

There was nothing luxurious about the *Tide.* There was no bar, open buffet, casino, TV or theater, swimming pool, waiters to provide room service, and no personal deck or patio just outside the cabin. The *Tide* did have a cabin with a set of metal bunk beds with a reading light for each bed, an overhead light for the cabin proper, a single metal desk, and two metal wall lockers. In fact, the entire cabin was constructed of metal, without a single piece of wooden furniture or wooden trim that routinely adorns ocean liners and cruise ships. The metal had been painted a solid color; not a white or off-white or even Navy gray, but an unpleasant pale green, paler than a green apple or green tomato.

Thankfully, the cabin came with its own toilet and shower, and because the *Tide* was a steamship (the *SS* in the name stands for steamship), hot water was always available. As visually unappealing and austere as these accommodations were, this was to be home for more than a week, longer than I had been in New York City.

Despite its Spartan appearance, both the cabin's space and utility were sufficient for two people to endure for more than a week at sea. I say "two people" because the young Englishman who I had met the previous Friday, the day I bought my ticket, was to be my roommate during the crossing.

The twenty-two-year-old Martin Evers stood less than six feet tall, had an average build, dark black hair, and a tanned, ruddy complexion. He was tanned because for many months he had been doing outdoor labor. He lived just outside of London and was returning home. For the last three years and five months, he had been working his way around the world. When he went to a place, if he liked it, he stayed. If he didn't like it, he left. And when he ran out of money, which he said was often, he worked until he had saved up enough to move on. He worked several jobs in various cities in both Australia and the United States, but wages for manual labor in most other countries he visited were too low to save money. He didn't provide details, but I surmised he left home under less than ideal circumstances, because his excitement about returning home after being gone for nearly three and half years seemed tempered and reflective.

Two other paying passengers were onboard the *Tide*—a retired couple, Mr. and Mrs. Wendell Thorn who lived in Washington, D. C. To save the expense of shipping a car to England, they were buying a new car (a Ford) in England and were headed there to get it. Their final destination, as incredible as it may seem, was

Bethlehem and the Holy Land. They were driving all the way to the Holy Land from England. All my worries were over—all I had to do was catch the mother of all rides! Well, I didn't ask them if I could tag along and they didn't volunteer. Besides, they said the paperwork for the new car was going to take them many days to complete. Moreover, if I hitchhiked as fast in Europe as I had getting from Holcomb to New York City; I'd beat the Thorns to Bethlehem by plenty.

Two things about the Thorns remain crystal clear in my memory. One, they were excellent bridge players. They routinely shellacked Martin and me in a rubber or two of bridge each evening after dinner. The second thing, and it meant absolutely nothing to me at the time, was their part-time job to supplement their retirement income. During the daytime, they watched three children for a twenty-five-year veteran Congressman and his wife from Grand Rapids, Michigan: Representative Gerald Ford and his wife Betty. Nine years later, Ford became the 38th President of the United States, the only person to hold both the Presidency and Vice-presidency without being duly elected by the Electoral College.

Since we had left the dock at Brooklyn Army Base late at night, the earliest opportunity to see the expanse of the Atlantic Ocean was early the next morning, but no luck. An hour or two before sunrise, we became enveloped in a thick fog. Even with the advanced use of radar, maritime law requires ships to blast their foghorns regularly during periods of limited visibility.

We were way too far south to hit an iceberg and suffer the same consequences as the *Titanic*, but loudly announcing our presence to other ships at sea greatly increased our chance of avoiding a collision. Without missing a beat, the *Tide* unremittingly boomed her annoying foghorn every one minute and forty-five seconds for nearly thirty hours!

The captain stated with the fog and the absence of wind, he had never seen calmer seas this far north. The sea was smooth enough we barely perceived the ship's movement. I tested the smoothness by successfully building a house of cards on the dining room table. The calmness helped us make excellent speed, just over fifteen knots an hour—about eighteen miles an hour. At this rate, we might make the crossing to England in seven days. Once we cleared the influence of land, the Newfoundland peninsula specifically, the fog should lift, winds should increase, and the seas should become much rougher. They did.

Encased in fog and with nothing to see, I decided it was a good time to do my laundry, untouched since I had left Kansas eleven days earlier. Under the incessant annoyance of the foghorn, Martin and I turned the cabin into a laundromat, ate supper at 5:00 p.m., got beat badly in bridge by the Thorns, and turned in about midnight, both hoping to see the Atlantic the next day.

When we awoke the next day, we saw the ocean. Even with the sky solidly overcast without the slightest ray of sunshine, the magnitude, the vastness, and sheer immensity of the ocean almost defied description. Having been born and raised in southwest Kansas, I had never seen expanses of water beyond a few small lakes. Most lakes were small enough I could wave across to people on the opposite shore. With only four-to-six foot swells and few whitecaps, the monotony of the ocean water stretched unendingly in every direction. What I remember best about seeing the ocean for the first time—and this may be true for many people—is how it made me feel small and insignificant. I watched the ocean from the sun deck for a few minutes and then took a stroll on all four sides of the ship—port, starboard, bow, and stern. From every direction, the view was always the same—a seemingly never-ending expanse of water.

I had waited a lifetime for this sight and after thirty minutes, I was thoroughly bored. Without seeing other ships or animals such as whales, porpoises, or even sea gulls, we faced a long and boring ride to England. The boredom was broken temporarily when just before noon the captain called for an abandon-ship drill, commonly called a life-boat drill, surprisingly two full days after we left port. Despite the fact that neither of the motors on the two life-boats would start, all four of us landlubbers passed muster. After some reading, I ironed the jeans I had washed the day before, had supper with Martin, the Thorns, and the ship's captain, played a full evening of bridge, and went to bed just after midnight.

We traversed the western third of the Atlantic. The middle third was as monotonous and routine as the first days had been. Skies remained cloudy—almost the color of steel. On two days, rain fell steadily; not rain from a storm, but a cold, chilling, steady rain more associated with late fall than with the first few weeks of summer. Still, the food was good in both quality and quantity and everyone was getting plenty of rest.

Saturday, June 12 th, was my paternal grandparents' fiftieth anniversary. I sent them a telegram from the ship, passing on best wishes. Regretfully, I missed the big family get-together and particularly missed seeing my aunts and uncles and many cousins. I was the only grandchild absent. In the 1950s and into the 1960s, our family was close and we frequently met on Sunday afternoon at our grandparents' house to visit, play, and eat watermelon. Of course, grandpa always brought over a horse or two from the farm and gave the kids rides, often three or four kids on one horse. It was all great fun in those days and I got melancholy thinking about missing the event. However, the summer of '65 was the only summer available for my extended trip. The next two summers I trained for combat in the Army and the summer after that, I put my training to use as a Field Artillery officer in South Vietnam.

The final third of the crossing was far more note-worthy than the earlier days had been. On the seventh day out, we finally saw the sun. The wind increased and the white-capped waves reached six to ten feet. The ship tossed and rolled with rougher seas, but not enough to make us queasy. The taste of sea salt on my lips was a unique experience. We also saw westbound ships more frequently and sighted both whales and porpoises as well.

As we prepared for our final turn northeastward to Southampton, a miscommunication occurred between the captain and the helmsman. We were supposed to turn northeast to 029°, but somehow we turned to 229°. For about five minutes, we headed directly for South America! The captain and the crew quickly realized their mistake, but not before we got crossways with the high seas and pitched and rolled and yawed in every direction. For fifteen minutes, we bounced like a slow-motion bucking bronco as high waves splashed over the deck—the best ride I'd had since the rides at the World's Fair.

We had no sooner resumed our correct course then we changed course again. The captain received word a dock strike had begun in Southampton and no dock workers would unload our cargo. We were diverted and scheduled to dock and unload in Saint-Nazaire, France. The crossing would be extended by at least one more day, possibly two. Coming through the Bay of Biscay, we encountered fifteen-to-twenty-foot seas and gale-force winds. The poor sailing conditions delayed our arrival at Saint-Nazaire until 7:00 p.m.—just enough to miss the evening's high tide. Consequently, we anchored in the harbor and waited for the high tide the next morning. With much advice from Martin, I spent the evening packing, discarding unnecessary items, and then re-packing my suitcase for the extensive travels ahead.

While packing, I asked Martin if he had ever thought

about quitting his world travels and going home sooner. He thought about it a few times, but he always changed his mind about going home early. He had never had the money (before now) to return home on his own, and he didn't want to ask the British Consulate to ship him home. They would have shipped him home alright—but at their convenience—and he would still have to pay them back after he returned. He thought it better to just stick to his original plan of making his own way. I admired him for his commitment and was glad to have the information about the option of the government sending a traveler home. I didn't plan to have the government send me back, but if I ever got into a real financial bind, it could be an option.

Early the next day, I awoke to the sound and movement of a tugboat pushing us into position toward the docks in Saint-Nazaire. Even though Saint-Nazaire boasts a major harbor at the mouth of the Loire River, the port is shallow, requiring the ship to go through a series of locks. We docked shortly after breakfast. Soon thereafter, French immigration and customs officials came on board to stamp our passports and to ensure we weren't bringing in drugs, contaminated fruit, or too much money (fat chance of that!)

I cannot imagine the logistical nightmare for people or companies looking for their goods to be delivered to England and those goods winding up in France. But for passengers, since our tickets stated we were to be delivered to England—Southampton specifically—the captain was certain the ship would pay our way. He thought we would go to Paris by train and then take an airplane to London. The captain had no sooner given us his words of assurance when a United States Lines representative boarded the ship and laid out the plan to get us from Saint-Nazaire back to England. The captain was partly right. Martin and I were to take a train from Saint-Nazaire to Paris, a train from Paris to Dieppe, France, a boat from Dieppe to New Haven, England, and another train to London. That was the good news. The bad news was we had to endure another insufferable night on board the ship.

Earlier, French immigration officials had stamped our passports, so consequently, we were cleared to leave the ship. Just after the noon meal on board, I did exactly that. On the afternoon of Thursday, June 17th, 1965, I stepped on foreign soil for the first time. My first overseas country was France and my second continent was Europe. I was elated! I felt I had accomplished something. For a couple of hours, I walked the streets of Saint-Nazaire, stopping to buy postage stamps and a pocket-size English-to-French dictionary. I returned to the ship in time for supper—my last meal on board ship—and cheerfully looked forward to my last night on the *SS Pioneer Tide*.

From the time the ship left Brooklyn Army Base at 10:45 p.m. on June 7th until we tied up at Saint-Nazaire on June 17th, nine and half days had passed. I slept on board the *Tide* for thirteen nights.

On Friday morning, June 18th, Martin and I left the ship early to catch a 7:17 a.m. train to Paris.

Paris and London

For nearly two weeks on board the *Tide*, Martin's stories of travel and adventure dazzled me. He held an even greater influence on me over the next two days as we traveled to Paris and London.

Except for the scenery, the 275-mile train ride from Saint-Nazaire to Paris was uneventful. French farmland looked greener than America's Midwest and more lush than anything I had seen growing up on the plains. In southwest Kansas, except for early spring and after heavy rains, everything was brown, yellow, and dry— particularly the Sand Hills south of Holcomb and Garden City. The verdant fields of France, including my first sight of vineyards, were in stark contrast to the often desert-like conditions of the southwest Kansas, the Texas and Oklahoma panhandles, and the eastern halves of Colorado and New Mexico. Early historians labeled the south-western plains as the "Great American Desert" and American farmers settled both coasts and many other states before settling on the plains. Still, with the discovery of the Ogallala Aquifer, one of the world's largest underground water tables, coupled with the advent of irrigation, western Kansas produced bumper crops—as long as a little rain came and the underground water held out. During the height of the Dust Bowl in the

1930s and long before irrigation became commonplace, rain was intermittent at best. Thousands of area farmers lost everything. As I scooted along in a train at sixty miles an hour through the verdant French countryside, I found it difficult to imagine such a tragedy ever happening in France. The French countryside was not only beautiful, but highly productive as well. No wonder the Germans tried to steal it twice in the twentieth century!

Another fascinating aspect of French crop production caught my eye. In the US, tens of thousands of acres of potentially productive cropland is wasted along America's highway and railroad right-of-ways. Not so in France. In France, those living along the railroad tracks take full advantage of right-of-way land adjacent to their property. Many landowners grow garden vegetables between the railroad ties right up to the steel railroad tracks. Tubular crops such as beets, radishes, turnips, radishes, and carrots grew perfectly well, apparently without being stunted in any way by speeding trains passing every few hours. Naturally, with garden land being much more scarce in the suburbs, this practice of track-side planting was more common there than in the countryside.

Three weeks earlier, I had gone through Indianapolis, Indiana one day before the Indianapolis 500 was held. On the way to Paris, we went through Le Mans, France a day before the running of the *24 Heures du Mans* auto race. Race fans would die for the opportunity to see both races, particularly in the same year. But, I was a baseball fan and auto racing didn't interest me. Consequently, that was the closest I ever got to a Formula 1 Race.

Martin and I arrived at the Paris train depot at 12:30 p.m. Trains left Paris for Dieppe regularly and on to England, but Martin wanted to look around Paris for a while. We stashed our luggage in a locker at the train station and hurried out to see as much of the city as possible in a single day. Visitors can see much of Paris and enjoy the ambiance of the city by walking around and looking at the historic sites and that's just what we did. We walked up and down the city streets and rode the subway just as I had in New York City.

We walked the famous Avenue des Champs-Élysées with its high-priced cinemas, cafés, and clothing shops. The Champs-Élysées, the most famous street in Paris, boasts some of the most expensive real estate in the world. In that vein, Champs-Élysées real estate compares favorably to Fifth Avenue in New York City and Russell Street in Hong Kong. We walked to the west end of Champs-Élysées to see the Arc de Triomphe. The arch honors those who fought and died for France in the French Revolutionary War and the Napoleonic Wars. We also visited the Opera House, the church of Notre Dame, and, of course, the Eiffel Tower.

The only place we paid to visit was the Louvre on the right bank of the Seine. The Louvre is an historic building in its own right and houses one of the world's largest art museums. Even though I was liberal arts major in college, I studied American history, not art. Truthfully, without the guide and the brochure, I didn't know the difference between a Titian and a Rembrandt or between a Picasso and an El Greco. Despite my shortcomings in art appreciation, I enjoyed the paintings, sculptures, and other historic artifacts.

When we left Saint-Nazaire for Paris earlier in the day, I wasn't convinced I was going to England. If cashing in my $13.50 train/boat ticket to London was an option, I'm certain I would have forgone England on this trip. But, I couldn't sell my ticket, and Martin really wanted me to go to London with him. Most assuredly, I would have skipped London without his persuasion. Having been in Paris less than ten hours, we boarded a train at 10:04 p.m. for the 120-mile trip to Dieppe.

At two in the morning, we boarded a ferry for the sixty-mile trip across the British Channel to New Haven. All the stories about the rough seas in the British Channel are true. We bounced up and down and rolled sideways like a fishing cork. Sleep was impossible. Several passengers got sick. I turned as green as a gourd but Martin saved me, just barely, when he passed me a couple of motion-sickness pills. The nausea was ten times worse than anything I had felt aboard the *Tide* and I was totally miserable for the entire three-and-a-half-hour trip. Never before (or since) have I ever been so happy to touch land.

Whether from the seasickness, the pills, or lack of sleep, I was still queasy on land. Since I felt terrible, I naturally got a British Immigration Officer who wanted my life's history. Among other questions, he asked me where I was staying in the short term, where I was going to live in England in the long term, whether or not I was going to seek work in England, and how much money I brought with me. After an endless barrage of questions, he realized my presence was no threat to England's safety. He stamped my passport and directed me to the train to London.

Martin was pensive and quiet as we rode the train on the last leg of his around-the-world journey. He hardly spoke a word since he flipped me the Dramamine. I understood his being emotional about going home after being away for such a long time, but his demeanor was more anxious and apprehensive than joyous. I didn't interrupt his thoughts and we arrived without fanfare at London's Victoria train depot at 7:30 a.m. Sadly, no friend or family member was there to meet him. We said a clumsy good-bye and that we hoped our paths would cross again. We both knew they never would. He walked out of the train station and that was the last time I saw him. I was on my own again, so I sat there a few minutes contemplating my next move.

Being dog-tired from lack of sleep while crossing the channel, I decided to look for a youth hostel. Passengers on the ferry told me that youth hostels, found in almost every good-size city in Europe, were the least expensive place to spend the night. I quickly found the nearest hostel, but it was already full for the night. London had two other hostels and they were both full as well. In addition, I had to join the youth hostel association in order to stay at a hostel and the membership fee was $6.00. With all of London's hostels fully occupied, procrastinating on membership seemed the best option at the time.

I checked out two or three hotels and each was $3.75 to $4.50, which I thought was expensive. After grabbing some pastries for breakfast, I felt much better, so I returned to the train depot and stored my suitcase. I decided to explore London in much the same manner Martin and I had done in Paris the day before.

From the train station, a short walk took me to Westminster Abbey. I was fascinated by the church's Gothic architecture with pointed arches and flying buttresses—architecture I'd never seen anywhere in America. I was even more impressed, however, by the tombs of famous English people, probably because the realistic effigies atop many of the tombs depicted what the person looked like at the height of their glory. I had not taken any English history courses, but I sat through a college class on English literature and recognized the names of some of the authors and poets buried at the abbey: Chaucer, Shakespeare, Pope, Milton, and Dickens, among others. Composer George Frederic Handel and scientist Sir Isaac Newton, who "discovered" gravity, are also buried there. Of the many sites I saw in New York, Paris, and London, Westminster Abbey was the most impressive.

I walked to the Parliament Building and the Tower of Big Ben then crossed the Thames River on the London Bridge. There have been several historic London bridges, but the bridge I crossed that day was completed in 1831. The 1831 bridge and several predecessors were the object of the nursery rhyme and singing game, "London

Bridge Is Falling Down." Before this 135-year-old bridge fell down, the city of London sold it to an American investor. The bridge was dismantled in 1967, moved across the Atlantic Ocean and through the Panama Canal, then reassembled block-by-block in Lake Havasu City, Arizona.

After riding the London subway for an hour or so— my third subway in three major cities—I caught a train for a short ride to the Royal Botanic Gardens, Kew, in the southwest corner of London. Even though I had no background in agronomy or botany, I always had an interest in trees. At home, we had two types—Chinese elm and cottonwood. Occasionally I'd see a few fruit trees such as peach, pear, or apple, but other than that and the few conifers I'd seen on our trips to the Rockies, it was always the same old boring elm or cottonwood. I was sure a visit to Kew would enlighten me.

Once I arrived, I saw the display of trees and plants was far too great for me to see in a short visit. Through an on-site brochure, I discovered the Kew gardens existed since 1759 and housed the world's largest collection of living plants. It would take me days to see everything there—a challenge more difficult than seeing everything in baseball's hall of fame in five minutes. I wish I could say I saw most of the plants and trees at Kew; but I did not. I was duly impressed, however, by the magnificence of the many plants and trees I did see. It was after dark and impossible to read the placards showing each plant's English description and scientific (Latin or Greek) equivalent when my two-hour visit ended and I boarded a train to return to metropolitan London.

It was after 9:00 p.m. by the time I returned to the Victoria train station and retrieved my suitcase. Having been discouraged earlier in the day when trying to find a hotel room, I decided to take a train to Dover, England and spend the night there. But when I got to Dover, I thought I might as well book passage back across the channel to France. Maybe this time, the passage would be smoother and I would be able to sleep on the boat.

I intended to book passage to Calais, France, but the ferry wasn't going to Calais; it was going to Dunkirk instead. I bought a $7.00 ticket and hopped on board for the dreaded return across the Channel. On board, I met four fellow hitchhikers, two girls and two boys from three different countries. None of them were traveling together; all five of us met for the first time on the boat. Two were heading for Germany and Austria and two others to Europe's Nordic countries. (None were going nearly as far as the Holy Land.) The five of us had a wonderful three-hour conversation and, thankfully, none of us got sick. After my experience on the previous crossing, I was euphoric just to avoid the nausea and overall discomfort. We landed at Dunkirk about 12:30 a.m.

Before we landed, I asked the girls where they were staying after they got off the boat. They told me a man had offered to put them up for the night. The offer sounded ominous to me, but the man turned out to be a priest for the Church of England and he was returning to

France after visiting relatives. The girls introduced me and he kindly offered to put me up for the night as well. Since I had been without sleep for nearly two nights, I was thrilled with the offer. As it turned out, the priest had both a home and an Anglican church in Dunkirk. Since he was an Englishman, naturally he offered us a spot of tea, even though it was nearly 2:00 a.m. We drank the tea and went to bed in different rooms of the rectory.

I spent over ten hours in Paris and only a little longer in London and didn't spend the night in either place. Yet I felt I got as much out of the cities (or as much out of myself) as might be reasonably expected. I was happy I visited both cities, but knew full-well the circumstances might have turned out differently. If the *Tide* had not been diverted to France, I probably would have missed Paris. If I had never met Martin or failed to develop a friendship with him during the Atlantic crossing, I probably would have missed London. That said, I was pleased to have those beautiful cities and their wonderfully historic sites behind me, and anxiously looked forward to continuing my trip.

Belgium, Luxembourg, and Switzerland

I have no idea if being hosted by an Anglican priest and sleeping in a church rectory in Dunkirk was part of the divine inspiration I was seeking on this trip. But after the fast-paced, nearly non-stop travel I experienced during the previous forty-eight hours, sleeping was divine.

The priest continued his hospitality by providing us a breakfast of sweet rolls and more tea. By 10:00 a.m., however, I stood on the outskirts of Dunkirk, looking for a ride to Ostend, Belgium. Ostend is located in the Flemish province of West Flanders and is the largest city on Belgium's North Sea coast. My general plan was to go to Ostend, turn eastward to Brussels, then onward through Luxembourg, Switzerland, and into Italy.

It was Sunday, June 20th, and as I stood by the highway on the north side of Dunkirk, it occurred to me I had not hitchhiked for three weeks. In fact, I had covered 4,000 miles without a single mile of hitchhiking. Looking for a ride into Belgium got off to a slow start. With a handful of short rides, it took almost seven hours to go the thirty-odd miles to Ostend. Hell, as a marathoner, I could run that far in half the time—without a suitcase, of course. I felt terribly dejected and as it turned out, I spent more time on that stretch of road than on any other in Western Europe.

I didn't think too much about it at the time, but when I crossed from France to Belgium, I did so without going through customs or immigration from either country. Unlike the lengthy hassle I experienced when I landed in England, I crossed the border into Belgium as easily as crossing from Kansas to Colorado in my own car.

Sixty-eight miles of main thoroughfare ran between Ostend and Brussels, so I had little trouble getting a ride into Belgium's capital city. Thinking the hotels might be expensive, I stayed there only two hours until darkness fell, then took a city bus to the edge of town on the main road heading southeast toward Namur and Luxembourg. Several short rides brought me to the Belgium town of Aubange, just outside the Luxembourg border, where I stopped at a restaurant for a sandwich and Coca-Colas (Cokes). I also bought two postage stamps and while I ate and rested, I wrote letters home and left them at a hotel to be mailed the next day.

Although I spent little time in Paris and London, I left without regrets. Not so in Belgium. The country's rich but bloody wartime history, particularly during the last two centuries, belies its size and geographic location. Famous battles occurred in World Wars I and II in both Liege and Namur. More well-known were the Ardennes offensive and counter-offensive between the Germans and American troops in late 1944 and early 1945. Americans called this confrontation the "Battle of the

Bulge" and my Uncle Lavon had first-hand experience in the worst of the fighting there. The most famous battle in Belgium, however, occurred on June 18, 1815. On that date, Lord Wellington and British Allies defeated French Emperor Napoleon Bonaparte near the small town of Waterloo just outside of Brussels. I missed the 150th anniversary of the major event by only two days and wished I spent much more time in Belgium; specifically at the battlefield at Waterloo.

Belgium is a small country but Luxembourg is smaller, just slightly smaller than the state of Rhode Island. Once I dropped off the letters in Aubange, a short ride took me to the Luxembourg border and again I crossed into another country without checking in or out with immigration. Soon, I was in downtown Luxembourg, the capital. At nearly 3:00 a.m. and after a terribly long day—in time, not distance—I was ready to crash at the nearest hotel. I checked out three or four hotels without particularly caring about the price. As it turned out, price was irrelevant; all the hotels were full. At the fanciest hotel of the lot, the night clerk let me sit in a comfortable over-stuffed chair in the lobby where I slept soundly for two hours.

At 5:00 a.m., I was back on the road again with a general plan of leaving Luxembourg, going through north-eastern France, and getting into Switzerland before the day's end. In the same manner in which I crossed into Belgium and into Luxembourg, I crossed back into France without anyone checking or stamping my passport.

Once I was in France again, everything was okay, because my passport matched my location.

I had little difficulty catching rides between cities and I arrived in Metz, France in quick order. Fortune was with me because shortly after, I caught a lengthy ride to Strasbourg, France, the capital and principal city of the Alsace region in northeastern France and the ninth-largest city in the country. Both the city and the region of Alsace are historically German-speaking and I had a terrible time communicating with the people and getting on the correct bus to get me through the city. Many European cities, particularly those situated along rivers, seem to be two blocks wide and ten miles long. Strasbourg is much larger than that and, consequently, it took me over two hours to get through it.

The next major city in sight was Basel located in northwest Switzerland and I quickly covered the ninety miles from Strasbourg to Basel. French immigration stamped my passport never knowing (or caring) that I had been in Belgium or Luxembourg. Without undue questioning or fanfare, Switzerland immigration stamped my passport too making my status official and legal in Switzerland—the fifth country on my tour.

The city of Basel is situated on the Rhine River where the Swiss, French, and German borders meet. It has suburbs in all three countries, and although I spent several hours there during the afternoon, I never crossed the Rhine River from Switzerland into Germany. Germany was one of several countries I have seen from afar but never entered. Other countries included Albania, Israel, and Saudi Arabia on this trip, and three years later, Cambodia, Laos, and North Vietnam.

I thought getting through Strasbourg was bad; it took me twice as long to get through Basel; more than four hours. It's the third largest city in Switzerland, but the size wasn't the trouble—nobody I met spoke English. Everybody in Basel speaks German or French or a local variant of the Swiss German dialect called Basel German. As I found out later, many Swiss people in the southeast portion of the country speak Italian. Thankfully for us lazy Americans who disdain the idea of learning a foreign language, the universal travel language is English, including for those in the hitchhiking fraternity.

It was dusk when I left Basel and a few miles southeast, I stopped for the night in the small town of Leistal. Again, I had trouble communicating. When I tried to get a room at the hotel, I needed help from a fellow traveler who spoke Spanish. Thankfully, I paid attention during my Spanish language classes during the two previous years. Mr. Garruth Ruggles, a language professor from Mexico and an American military veteran, taught Spanish at Holcomb High School and both Spanish and French at the junior college in Garden City. I took both languages under his tutelage. With his guidance, I gained a solid foundation with Spanish, but my French never developed.

Every day in high school Spanish class, we tried to divert the daily lesson and coerce Mr. Ruggles into talking about his World War II experiences. We rarely succeeded except to find out he had been a Japanese prisoner for more than two years and survived the "Death March" of Bataan in the Philippines. As many as 10,000 Filipinos and 650 Americans died or were murdered along the route. Mr. Ruggles just said he was one of the lucky ones. He also told us he dreamt in both English and Spanish and as high school students, we thought that was cool.

So with the direct help of a fellow traveler and indirect help from my Spanish teacher, I got a bed, shower, and toilet—in three separate rooms, in German-speaking Leistal, Switzerland, for $3.00. I took a shower, my first since I had left the *Tide* four days earlier.

The shower and a full night's sleep in a real bed did wonders for my spirits and my morale. To top it off, breakfast was included with the price of the room—my first introduction to a European breakfast. Commonly known as a "Continental" breakfast, the food included all the bread and jelly I could eat and all the tea I could drink. At least it was filling. Before I left town, I used some remaining French francs to mail three letters, then cashed a $20 traveler's check leaving me with $140.

Just after 9:00 a.m., I headed for the Swiss capital of Bern and the beautiful Aar River that runs through it. The fast-moving 120 mile-long Aar is a tributary of the Rhine and is fed by a number of alpine glaciers. The river's water is the most beautiful light turquoise I had ever seen. With much enthusiasm, I worked my way through Bern's city streets fully enjoying the river's beauty as I walked many blocks along the river's banks. Albert Einstein worked out his theory of relativity while employed as a clerk at the Bern patent office. Unfortunately, I missed seeing him—by about fifty years or so.

I was now in the heart of the Swiss Alps. Few sights, either before that day or since, have impressed me with their beauty and grandeur more than the mountains of Switzerland. Neither the Rockies, the Andes, nor the foothills of the Himalayas are more grandiose than what God or Nature carved out in Switzerland. Each turn in the road presents another spectacular view of snow-capped mountains, crystal clear springs and brooks, and verdant meadows and pastures. Certainly the world is full of beautiful places, but I found the scenery in Switzerland consistently more breathtaking and memorable than any other place I've seen. To demonstrate the widespread belief that sometimes teenagers think they know it all, I wrote in my diary, "The US doesn't have any mountains." That utterly false statement was long before I saw the rugged Sierra Nevada Mountains and beautiful Mt. Whitney in California, the Grand Tetons near Yellowstone Park in Wyoming, and the snow-covered peak of Mt. McKinley in Alaska. That diary entry reflected my real ignorance and naiveté about American geography. But, at that time, I didn't know about those scenic American places and excitingly looked forward to the many beautiful miles of Swiss Alps still in front of me.

At the east edge of Bern, a middle-aged businessman wearing a suit and tie gave me a ride on his vintage BMW motor bike. As we sped through the Swiss countryside at sixty miles-per-hour, several drivers appeared highly amused when they saw me clutching my suitcase tightly with one hand and holding the biker's waist with the other. I was thankful for the ride, but happy and relieved to dismount from my precarious position when we stopped an hour later. At exactly 4:00 p.m., the biker let me off on a narrow two-lane road at the base of Grimsel Pass directly across from a hotel. Now this drop-off was convenience of the first order. I went into the hotel lobby and to my surprise, the young female clerk spoke English. I told her I didn't normally stop hitchhiking this early in the day, but if I couldn't catch a ride, I would be back to rent a room. She told me they had plenty of rooms, but the two or three hour trip to the top of the pass and back down on the other side might prevent me from being picked up that day. She thought if I didn't get a ride in a few minutes, I would unlikely get one until morning. She added most drivers don't attempt the pass at night since ice and snow frequently cover the road at higher elevations. I thanked her for the information and returned to my spot beside the road, knowing I had a solid back-up plan.

It was my lucky day. I had been waiting about ten minutes when a thirty-something businessman pulled over in a Volkswagen and offered a ride. When I got in, I was delighted that he spoke perfect English. He had made the trek to the top of Grimsel Pass and down the other side to Brig many times. He confirmed what the hotel clerk told me; regardless of the time of year, there was always a danger of freezing temperatures and ice covering the roadway near the top of the pass. He wanted someone to ride along with him in case he slid off the road and needed help digging the car out of a snow bank. If everything went well and we failed to encounter snow or ice, he thought we might reach Brig about sundown. We made our way slowly over the steep, winding road with each curve revealing more awe-inspiring scenery than the one before. During the previous two days, I saw deer on a few occasions, but as we made our ascent on Grimsel Pass, the driver pointed out a small group of ibex or chamois on a distant mountain side. The animals were so far away, he wasn't sure which animal it was. I'm certain I wouldn't have known the difference between the two if they ran directly in front of the car.

Once we got near the top, just as the driver warned, snow was piled everywhere. Snow banks were ten to twelve feet high on both sides of the road and thick ice flows dotted the two or three lakes near the top of the pass—and this was June 22nd! The driver told me snow always remained on Grimsel Pass since the pass seldom reaches temperatures of more than 45°. He added the pass was often closed from October until late June due to deep snow cover. Snowplows, however, try to keep the road open to allow access from Bern to Brig and to allow patrons to reach Hotel Grimselblick at the top of the pass. I found out much later that Grimsel Pass is only 7,103 feet in elevation, but the pass always has more snow than many mountain tops twice that high. The ancient Inca capital of Cuzco in Peru is situated in the Andes at more than 11,000 feet above sea level, yet snow is virtually

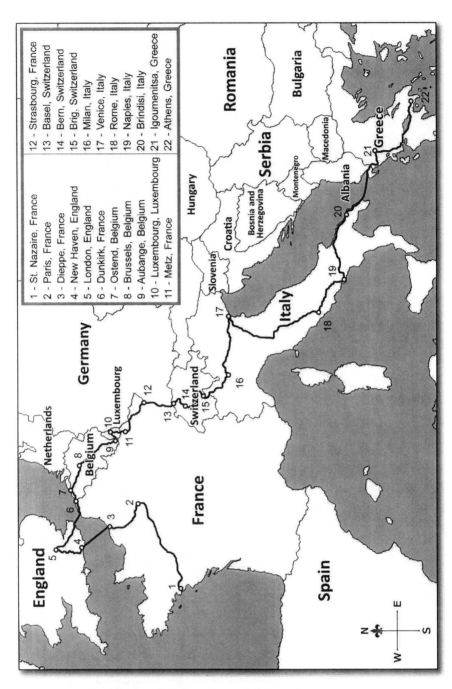

1 - St. Nazaire, France
2 - Paris, France
3 - Dieppe, France
4 - New Haven, England
5 - London, England
6 - Dunkirk, France
7 - Ostend, Belgium
8 - Brussels, Belgium
9 - Aubange, Belgium
10 - Luxembourg, Luxembourg
11 - Metz, France
12 - Strasbourg, France
13 - Basel, Switzerland
14 - Bern, Switzerland
15 - Brig, Switzerland
16 - Milan, Italy
17 - Venice, Italy
18 - Rome, Italy
19 - Naples, Italy
20 - Brindisi, Italy
21 - Igoumenitsa, Greece
22 - Athens, Greece

St. Nazaire, France to Athens, Greece

unheard of. Apparently, snowfall has more to do with continental location and weather patterns than elevation.

We safely zigzagged down the south side of the pass where the driver dropped me off in Brig just at sundown. He advised me to find a place to spend the night because the next high mountain pass was closed and wouldn't be open for traffic until morning. At a pastry shop, I grabbed some bread and a Coke then walked to the edge of town. Not far from a dim streetlight, I sat down in the soft grass of the barrow ditch by the road and made myself as comfortable as possible to spend the night. The night air was cool, but I kept warm using the bright yellow fleece warm-up top borrowed from the junior college track team.

A giant of a man who appeared to be a weight lifter or bodybuilder must have spotted me in the ditch from a nearby pub. At about 10:00 p.m., he offered me a lift on his hog—his Harley-Davidson motor cycle. He spoke no English and I had no idea where or how far we were going—or if he had ulterior motives. I knew the mountain pass was closed for the night so the ride had to be short. Turns out, he was a farmer and we drove to his place about a mile out of town where he let me sleep in his barn. So on my last night in Switzerland I slept quite comfortably on the soft hay in a barn with two milk cows and several chickens. As I said, it must have been my lucky day.

Italy, the Vatican, and on to Brindisi

When the farmer milked the cows early in the morning, I ignored him and slept another two or three hours in the soft hay. At 10:30 a.m., I stopped at the farmhouse to thank him for his hospitality and then walked the two hundred yards from the farm to the main road heading to Italy.

I soon got a ride with Mr. James Stillwell, a British Foreign Service officer stationed in Bonn, Germany who was heading to Italy. He knew how to speak and write four languages fluently (including Spanish) and was probably the most educated man I had met in my life; certainly the most educated I met on the trip. As required, we stopped at the Swiss-Italian border to check through immigration. In the immigration offices of most of the countries I visited, there was a special line for diplomats, politicians, and other VIPs. James quickly glided his way through the VIP line on both sides of the border and I conveniently tagged right along behind him.

Early in the afternoon, we stopped in a small Italian village and James bought dinner. We both had a large meal (is there any other size in Italy?) and he even induced me to try a glass of wine—my first. For the most part, I had been living on pastries and Cokes since I left the *Tide,* so I was grateful for the full meal, despite what I thought was an excessive amount of oils, vinegar, and garlic. After another hour or so, we arrived in Milan, James's destination on this trip. He was kind enough to drop me off at the eastern edge of the city.

The south edge of Milan was a more direct route to Rome, but I wanted to see Venice, a city that I had heard and read so much about. Admittedly, Venice was out of the way, but surely I could get from Venice to Rome. I counted on the adage that "All roads lead to Rome." This was true for two millennia, so it must be true in modern Italy.

Two rides from Milan brought me into the city of Venice, known for the beauty of its setting, architecture, and most prominently, its canals. With influence from both the Byzantine and Ottoman empires, the city's Gothic architecture is distinctive. Unlike smoothly rounded arches seen in much of the world's architecture, many buildings in Venice exhibit the Gothic lancet arch. Lancet arches are easy to spot and easy to identify—they have an acute point at the top like an arrowhead, a spearhead, or a lance. The arches on Westminster Abbey are similar, but the arches on the buildings in Venice are more pronounced and more pointed.

Despite the unusual architecture, the canals in Venice make the city unique. The city is situated in a marshy lagoon on more than a hundred small islands separated by these world-famous canals. Locals and tourists alike must use boats—primarily gondolas or water taxis—for transportation. I kept thinking Venice would be a most romantic place for a honeymoon. In fact, thousands of newlywed European couples choose Venice for that very thing. I observed scores of gondolas during the afternoon and evening I spent there, each gondola occupied by a couple and piloted by a gondolier crooning Italian love songs. Surprisingly, the city didn't smell like sea water or stale lagoon water, but more like lilacs. The city fathers must have added something to the water or sprayed perfume in the air, for the city not only looked good, but smelled great.

Just for the fun of it, I rode around a few minutes in a gondola with six other people who were not on their honeymoon. I also rode in water taxis from one part of the city to another. For a major tourist site, I found Venice's prices for taxis, souvenirs, and dry goods to be remarkably inexpensive. I priced some mohair sweaters which likely cost $15.00 to $20.00 in America, but were only $3.00 in Venice. I spent the night there in a modest hotel for only $2.48; a real bargain in a resort city. Again, I wrote letters home, left them for mailing at the hotel, and got a good night's rest in a bed.

I began to discover some days are better for hitch-hiking than others. Perhaps luckier is a better word. I left Venice at 9:00 a.m. with my destination—the Italian capital of Rome—some 350 miles away. Ten hours later, I was still about 100 miles outside the city and was certain I was destined to sleep by the roadway and finish the trip into Rome the next morning. With more than an hour's daylight left, I looked around for a good spot in a vineyard near the highway, but far enough away from the road where I couldn't be seen by passing cars. As I began walking away from the road and into the vineyard, a car stopped and offered a ride.

A married couple, an Italian husband and Finnish wife, was returning to their house in Rome after buying a new car in Bologna. And, they drove it like it was a new car, too—forty to forty-five miles an hour and no more. After a long day, the pace was agonizingly slow, yet I thoroughly enjoyed the panorama of the Italian countryside as the sun faded from the horizon. The slowness of my travel that day tried my patience, but I enjoyed seeing the farmland and vineyards of Italy as much as I had the farmlands of western France a few days earlier. Italy appeared less green, or at least the country was less green during late June when I passed through as many wheat fields had turned golden and were ready for harvest. Throughout the Italian countryside from Venice to Rome, the landscape conjured up thoughts of the ancient Roman Empire rather than the farmland of modern Italy. No doubt those thoughts were influenced by countless movies I saw depicting Roman Empire topography.

Without anything negative happening to their new car, the couple dropped me off in Rome where I quickly found a hotel for $1.92. Seemingly, the farther I got from America and the farther I got from Western Europe, the less expensive the accommodations. Generally speaking, this was true throughout the trip.

Each time I wrote a letter home, I asked my folks and

my girlfriend to write back "in care of general delivery" at the post office of a major city where I was headed. Rome was the first city I asked them to send letters. However, I was hitchhiking so fast and covering the miles so quickly it would have been nearly impossible for me to receive letters in Rome. Nonetheless, I left my hotel room at 8:00 a.m. and was at Rome's main post office by 9:00 a.m. Not surprisingly, there were no letters waiting for me, so I vowed to check tomorrow.

Just as I had in Paris and London, I walked about the city of Rome trying to see as much as possible on a limited budget. The first place I went was to Vatican City, an enclave and independent nation—the smallest nation in the world—completely surrounded by the city of Rome. Most of the Vatican was closed to the public and the Swiss Guards closely watched the gates. Still, I was able to see some parts of the Vatican without entering the complex itself, such as St. Peter's Square and Basilica and the Sistine Chapel. The Basilica of Saint Peter is the centerpiece of the Vatican and its magnificent marble cupola dominates the Rome skyline. Due to its historical, artistic, and religious significance, millions of people, (many of them non-Catholic), visit the seat of the Roman Catholic Church each year. In the summer of '65, I was one of them. Having seen Westminster Abbey only a week before, I judged the Vatican architecture far more impressive.

Next, I visited the Colosseum (or Coliseum) of Rome, the iconic symbol of Imperial Rome and one of modern Rome's most popular tourist attractions. Completed in

AD 80, the Colosseum is considered a great work of Roman architecture and engineering and was once capable of seating 80,000 spectators. In its glory days, the Colosseum was used for animal hunts, re-enactments of famous battles, and dramas based on Classical mythology. Although untrue, Hollywood has movie goers believing only executions and gladiatorial contests were held there, many between hungry lions and devoted but helpless Christians. As I stood there at the highest level in the Colosseum, I couldn't help but wonder how many Christians had died there needlessly.

For most visitors to Rome, the Vatican and the Colosseum might be the highlight of their trip. Others marvel at the architecture, scores of fountains and pools, and dozens of religious sites. Not me. Late in the afternoon I dashed off to Stadio Olimpico or the Olympic Stadium, where the summer Olympic Games were held in August and September of 1960. These were the first summer games to be covered by American, Canadian, and Mexican television, although I didn't see the games live since we had no TV. (We didn't get a TV until the spring of 1964 when I was a senior in high school. I was the last student in my class to do so.) I had seen replays, however, of the titanic struggle in Rome for the decathlon title between two University of Southern California classmates and friends, Rafer Johnson and C.K. Yang. Johnson won the gold. And what marathoner could forget Abebe Bikila of Ethiopia running bare-footed and winning the marathon to become the first black African Olympic champion?

The day I visited the stadium, no activities were taking place; no track and field events, no official soccer games, and none of the pick-up games among kids seen everywhere in Europe. And there were no visitors but me. A gate was open and I made my way down to the track and slowly walked a full lap around the stadium. Physically, I was there, but I was lost in my daydream about the grandeur of the Games. I thought of Billy Mills, a Native American and Kansas University student who had shocked the running world when he won the 10,000 meter run at the 1964 Olympics in Tokyo. No American had won that event before and none have won it since.

I thought of my home state of Kansas and the distance-running legacy at Kansas University. Three famous runners immediately came to mind. Glenn Cunningham, from Elkhart, Kansas in the far southwest corner of the state, whose legs were so badly burned they said he would never walk again. In the 1930s, Cunningham held the world record for the mile and flirted with breaking the four-minute barrier. Harold Hadley, from tiny Shallow Water, Kansas, fewer than twenty miles from my home town, was the first collegian to break the nine-minute barrier for two miles indoors. Most famous, however, was Wichita, Kansas miler and later Congressman Jim Ryun, who was the first high school boy to break the four-minute mile. I had competed in both cross-country and track meets against the latter two, admittedly well behind them.

I love baseball, but I love the running events in the Olympics equally as well. And I vowed as I walked around the Olympic Stadium in Rome on a perfect June evening under a beautiful sunset, to attend a summer Olympiad sometime in my lifetime. The next summer games were in Mexico City in 1968, but by then I had another job—fighting the North Vietnamese Army. A dozen years later, I paid for airfare, hotel rooms, and tickets for most of the track and field events at the Moscow Olympics in 1980. But alas, President Jimmy Carter told the Russians if they didn't leave Afghanistan, America wouldn't allow their Olympians to compete in Moscow. The Russians didn't leave, Carter kept his word, and I—along with hundreds of heart-broken American Olympians—didn't go to Moscow.

It was well after dark when I made my way back to my hotel room. I tossed and turned fitfully as I dreamed of running the 10,000 meters at the Mexico City Olympics in 1968.

I slept late, checked out of the hotel, and headed straight for Rome's main post office, with faint hope of getting a letter or two from home. No letters had arrived, so I asked the clerk to forward my letters to general delivery in Athens, Greece. That was the next major city on my trek, but I still had many miles to travel in Italy, plus I had to cross the Adriatic Sea and half of Greece. I left Rome with supreme confidence that by the time I arrived in Athens, letters would be waiting for me.

I left Rome late Saturday morning on June 26th. Immediately, I got one of the best rides on my entire trip. A man took me from Rome to ten miles south of Salerno, Italy, a distance of 180 miles. We bypassed Naples, but passed close enough to see Mount Vesuvius. The famous volcano has erupted off and on throughout much of the last one hundred years, but the most well-known eruption occurred in AD 79 when the volcano buried the cities of Herculaneum and Pompeii.

From Naples and Salerno on Italy's west coast (bordering the Tyrrhenian Sea), I turned inland across the Apennine Mountains toward Brindisi on the Adriatic Sea. From Rome to Brindisi is a long trip for a single day and I didn't make it. About halfway across the "boot" of Italy, a driver dropped me off on the east side of Matera, an ancient Italian town thought to originate from a prehistoric settlement and conceivably the first human settlement in Italy. I waited for a ride for two hours then gave up once darkness fell. In a nearby hay field, I found a spot to bed down for the night and was made more comfortable with the small, fleece blanket I had "borrowed" from the Rome hotel room earlier that day.

I suspect most hitchhikers wake up early whenever they sleep outside in a field or barrow ditch or similar environs. I know I always did. That morning outside of Matera, an early start gained me almost five miles in three hours. Quite discouraged, I gradually reached the next small village where I waited for a bus. For fifty-five cents, I contentedly rode the next sixty miles to the commercial and military port town of Taranto on the Ionian Sea, part of the much larger Mediterranean Sea. Once I arrived in Taranto outside the city limits, it took me only two rides to get across the Italian Peninsula to

Brindisi. The first ride left me about fifteen miles short of the city. The second ride, from two Italian men on vacation who just happened to be going to Greece too, took me directly to the dock where ships depart for Greece.

For $11, I purchased passage to cross the Adriatic Sea on the Hellenic-Mediterranean Lines' car-ferry *Appia*. Unfortunately, the ship wasn't scheduled to leave until late evening so I spent the afternoon and early evening walking around the city. I stopped at a sidewalk café for food and drinks, wrote letters home, then watched several old men play bocce ball—a game inherited from ancient Rome and popular in Italy and anywhere Italian immigrants congregate. The game has aspects of bowling, croquet, horseshoes, and curling, but between the language barrier and my inability to grasp the game's concept, I never figured it out.

In the early darkness of that Sunday evening in Brindisi as I waited for the *Appia* to depart, I thought of the slave rebel Spartacus and the movie by the same name. According to the movie, Spartacus, too, had paid for ship's passage from Brindisi, but the Roman Army bribed the pirates of Cilicia and he was double-crossed. Spartacus was trapped against the sea with no place to go and the Romans consequently defeated him. I missed being in the same place as Spartacus by about two thousand years, but I would not miss my boat—it left for Greece at 10:30 p.m.

Happy Days in Greece

I quickly cleared both customs and immigration into Greece without pomp and circumstance and was standing by the road outside the Greek port town of Igoumenitsa by 9:30 a.m. looking for rides to cover the 300 miles to Athens.

Unbeknownst to me because I had slept soundly for nearly eight hours onboard ship and failed to strike up a conversation with anyone, many travelers on the *Appia* were also heading for Athens. A number of them were fellow hitchhikers. After also clearing Greek immigration, eight or ten young people, including me, were milling around the same area trying to catch rides. Some were single and on their own, others were in groups of two, and three girls seemed to be together. Certainly, a "mob" of ten people in one spot is no way to hitchhike, so a few began walking down the main highway leading out of town.

The first person to catch a ride was a pretty French girl I noticed on the ship but hadn't spoken to. She had a pixie haircut and wore a sleeveless shirt and no bra. She also didn't shave her underarms—the first time I noticed that on a woman. Perhaps if I had been more observant of women's armpits in Paris I might have noticed, but I didn't. Later, I found out that unlike American women, many European women, particularly those from France and Germany, do not shave their underarms. Despite her hairy underarms, or perhaps because of them, the French girl quickly got a ride and left the rest of us standing there wishing to be so lucky.

The three girls traveling together ambled down the road and about fifteen minutes later, a truck stopped—it appeared that they caught a ride. For some reason though, perhaps for lack of room in the cab, the truck driver left the girls behind. When the truck left, I walked up and introduced myself. While the four of us waited for a ride, we visited at length and became friends.

The three girls, full-grown women really, were friends from England who lived outside London and worked as nurses in the same hospital. All three of them—Grace, Taz, and Judy—were twenty-three years old, much older than me. They were on "holiday," the British word for vacation, and were hitchhiking together from England to Athens. They had three weeks to travel and were scheduled to return to England by airplane from Athens.

Grace was the shortest of the group with a medium build and straight, long blond hair. Taz was taller with chipmunk-colored hair that hung loosely around her neck. She was the only one of the three who wore glasses. Judy was much heavier than either of the other two, possibly thirty-five to forty pounds overweight, with a full, Rubenesque figure and short-cropped brown hair. All three women were reasonably attractive, but Grace was the best-looking of the three. Each carried their belongings in rucksacks with a rolled-up sleeping bag beneath.

Undoubtedly, they thought I was crazy for hitchhiking with a suitcase. They seemed to be having a good time together and were far more patient than me. They didn't seem to mind too much about the long delay in getting out of town. I talked with Martin many days on board the *Tide,* but much of his English accent must have worn off during the years and months he had been gone from home. Not so with the three English nurses; I enjoyed listening to their British accents immensely.

Shortly after mid-day, (more than a three-hour wait), an Englishman stopped and picked up all four of us. That was the good news. The bad news is he took us a scant thirty miles and left us at the edge of a small Greek village in the mountains. We waited there another three hours drawing much attention from both kids and adults alike. We felt we were like pandas or baby hippos in a zoo. Late in the afternoon, a truck full of bags of concrete stopped and took us to a good-size town. We took time to have sandwiches and drinks and then, just about sundown, we trudged to the east edge of town. None of us were crazy about hitchhiking at night, so we walked about three-quarters of a mile out of town and spotted a hay field where we bedded down for the night.

While we walked to the field, some Greek soldiers, possibly National Guardsmen or Reservists, spotted us from their bivouac across the road. Two soldiers came over and visited and in broken English advised us they'd take us all the way to Athens by truck. They weren't leaving, however, until 8:00 p.m. Something must have gotten lost in translation, because it was almost 8:00 p.m. already. Maybe they meant 8:00 a.m. the next day. The truth was, the soldiers had something else in mind and there was probably never going to be a ride to Athens in military trucks. Not long after dark, Judy and a Greek soldier slipped off a few yards away. Meanwhile, the other two women and I selected a spot for the night. The women rolled out their sleeping bags and with me between the two of them, I got as comfortable as possible with my college sweat top and the light blanket I had used two nights earlier.

Now, it's common knowledge if not scientific fact that sounds carry over water for great distances. I can attest that on a windless, starry night in Greece, when it's quiet enough to hear an ant walking on sand, the sounds of lovemaking carry clearly for many yards over a Greek hay field. The three of us lay motionless in our makeshift beds pretending to be asleep, yet none of us were. What seemed like three hours but was probably half of that, Judy somehow found us in the dark and lay down on the other side of Grace. Remembering Judy's sexual encounter and thinking about the two "beautiful" women laying only an arm's length away from me, my groin ached mercilessly—and I spent a very uncomfortable and nearly sleepless night. With such prurient thoughts racing through my mind (and body), I was definitely a long way from any divine inspiration.

Morning couldn't arrive quickly enough, but it did eventually as it always does. As usual, I awoke early. This time, everything was damp and covered with dew. The women were still sleeping, so I left my suitcase and hiked back into town. A gas station attendant let me use the washroom to wash my face and use the bathroom. When I returned, the women were still asleep and I didn't bother them. Without my suitcase, I walked the forty or fifty yards to the main highway in hopes of flagging down a ride. At 7:00 a.m., a truck stopped and I relayed to him I wasn't alone and that three other people were with me. He must have been a local driver and had seen or heard about our appearance in town the night before, because he waited patiently as I rustled the women from their sleeping bags. Soon, the four of us were on our way to Athens.

Whether Greek drivers have a disdain for all hitch-hikers or whether they are simply uncomfortable about taking four of us at one time, I could not tell. But as I traveled toward Athens with the English women, the delays between rides were interminably long. The first driver took us well over a hundred miles, but after he let us off, it was more than three hours before our next ride: another truck. The second truck also took us over a hundred miles, but again, we had another three-hour wait. After only two rides and two three-hour waits, it was almost dark. Just as the night before, we began looking for a place (a field) to camp out for the night. About that time, a potato truck pulled over and offered us a ride to Athens. We were overjoyed, but knew we wouldn't get there until well after dark. True to his word, the driver took us all the way to Athens, but he stopped for an hour and added more potatoes to his load. Judy and Taz rode comfortably in the cab with the driver, but for Grace and I, riding on top of lumpy potato sacks was damp, cold, and uncomfortable. Sleep was impossible. We arrived in Athens at 2:30 a.m.—tired, sleepy, hungry, and thirsty.

We agreed it was too late to look for a hotel room, so we selected an all-night sidewalk café to pass the hours until morning. Judy and Taz rolled out their sleeping bags and lay down on top of them while Grace and I visited until 6:00 a.m., making her sleeping bag all but unnecessary. We discussed Soviet détente, the Kennedy assassination, and the declining strength of the Chinese yen, or something along those lines; I was too tired to remember exactly. What I do remember is the conversation between the women the second day was far less animated and far less spirited than it had been earlier. Whether Judy's encounter with the Greek soldier was a cause for disappointment or jealousy or other emotions—or for no reasons at all—the tenor and tone of their conversations were markedly changed.

We left the all-night café and walked to the main post office, arriving at 6:30 a.m., long before it opened. The women had some letters to mail and I was still hoping to get some letters from home. While we waited for the post office to open, we had breakfast at a nearby restaurant. Every Greek male within eyesight stared at the women as if they had never seen one before. As I soon discovered, women traveling without the accompaniment of men are extremely rare in that part of the world.

The women mailed their letters and I suffered another disappointing day at the post office—still no letters from home. To be less encumbered as we looked for a hotel, the four of us went to the Athens train station and checked our luggage. We found separate hotels about two blocks apart, but I had another errand to run. I had heard I needed a visa to get into Turkey, so I made my way to the American Embassy. I was told to pick up the visa at the Turkish border, then returned to the hotel for a much-needed shower and nap.

I met the women again at 4:00 p.m. and we went to the Acropolis of Athens to see the Parthenon and the remains of other ancient Greek buildings on the high, rocky outcrop overlooking the city. Dating back to the fifth century BC, the entire area has great architectural and historic significance. Some 2500 years later, Greek architecture remains influential in municipal, state, and national building construction throughout much of the Western world. I spent two or three enjoyable hours just walking around the site with the three nurses. Each woman had a camera, and along with hundreds of other tourists, they took several pictures of the ancient ruins that make up the Acropolis.

After viewing magnificent Greek architecture until almost sunset, the four of us retired to a nice restaurant were we had an excellent Greek dinner in honor of Taz's twenty-fourth birthday. The women even talked me into having a glass of wine, my second on this trip—in two countries, no less. (This could be habit forming.) We were still exhausted from the night before, so we made an early evening of it and took a taxi to the women's hotel. There, we said good-bye, knowing full well we would never see one another again. I had spent three delightfully happy days traveling and talking with these friendly and amiable English nurses.

I was done with British female companionship for a while, but I was not done with Greece; not by a long shot. From the port city of Igoumenitsa where we disembarked from the *Appia*, we trekked eastward and then southeastward to get to Athens. To get out of Greece by land, I needed to go back north, almost northwest, and then work my way north-east and east through the vast open countryside toward the Turkish border. What I was doing in essence, was circumnavigating my way around the Aegean Sea. Crossing the Aegean by ship would have been much quicker but far more expensive, so I went to Turkey using the land route.

As usual, getting out of a big city, particularly when I couldn't read the road signs, was both frustrating and challenging. Getting out of a metropolis the size of Athens was typical. Even though I was getting low on money, after checking at the main post office and being disappointed one more time, I hailed a taxi at 9:00 a.m. to take me to the edge of the Athens city limits.

When I left home, my entire amount of traveling money was wrapped up in traveler's checks—all in twenty-dollar denominations. Once I left America, I tried never to cash more than a single check at a time, knowing

I would be stuck with money, especially coins, that I couldn't use in the next country. This was long before the advent of the Euro— thirty-four years before to be exact. Each country had its own currency—English pounds, French francs, Italian lire, and German marks were standard in those respective countries. Belgium, Luxembourg, and Switzerland had their own money too, but French francs or Italian lire were acceptable almost everywhere in those three smaller countries. In Greece, the monetary unit in 1965 was the same as it had been in Greece for more than two millennia—drachmas. When I passed through Greece, the value of drachmas was between fifteen or eighteen drachmas to the dollar.

I had a few drachmas in my suitcase and several other coins of various denominations from the countries I had visited. For some reason (and I don't remember why), I had a single five-dollar bill in my billfold and I decided to pay the Greek taxi driver using the five. I also don't recall the distance he took me to get out of town, but when I gave him the five, he refused to give me change. That five-dollar bill represented at least two night's stay in a hotel and probably some food as well. I grabbed my five from his hand and refused to pay him anything. Before I got out of the taxi, he sped off to the nearest police station with me in tow. None of the police spoke English, but they clearly understood why I was upset. The police sided with me and the taxi driver coughed up the proper change, in drachmas, of course. I hoarded them until I could put them to better use.

From the outskirts of Athens, I got two short rides covering only fifty miles, and was dropped off just outside a small village. I waited there almost three hours for the next ride. I mused over the idea that the long waits the nurses and I experienced during the three previous days had nothing to do with our four-person group. I concluded Greek drivers just don't like to pick up hitchhikers. Still, I had made it this far.

For us hitchhikers who don't like to walk, waiting in one spot for hours is tediously boring. Not as boring as crossing the ocean on a ship, but boring nonetheless. That day, the first of July, I was thoroughly bored as I waited outside the small Greek village. As I often did, I absentmindedly began throwing rocks across the road, at nothing in particular, probably a fence post. There were no houses or cars nearby nor anything else that was breakable as far as I could see. Nonetheless, my rock throwing didn't sit well with a slightly bent eighty-year-old Greek woman clad in black from top to bottom. She approached me with a switch and callously whacked me over the back of my legs two or three times. I don't know, but conceivably that was her field and she and her family had spent decades clearing out the stones. Clearly, she didn't want anyone throwing rocks back into her field. She briskly walked away and no more than five minutes later, she returned with the police. The policeman seemed mildly amused about the whole ordeal and through sign language, suggested I quit throwing rocks. I did.

A hundred miles down the road, I stopped to eat for the first time that day. The waiter charged me twelve drachmas for the meal—less than a dollar—but somehow I thought that was too much and stubbornly refused to pay. A big Greek bouncer grabbed me by the arms and at the same time sent a young boy to fetch the police. Since I was profoundly overmatched, I realized what a real bargain the meal had been, paid the amount in full, and quickly caught a ride before the police arrived.

At dusk, a driver in a slow-moving truck picked me up and we drove for four or five hours until well after midnight. In the middle of the Greek countryside, without a person, house, or town in sight, the driver pulled over. It wasn't sleep he was after; he was after me. Once he laid his hand on my shoulder, I grabbed my suitcase, jumped out of the truck, and ran along the highway for a half mile in the pitch black of night. Since the driver didn't follow me, either on foot or in his truck, I ducked onto the other side of the road beyond the barrow ditch and spent the rest of the night in a field.

Greece is the most mountainous country in Europe with less than thirty percent of the land suited for cultivation, mostly due to poor soil and rocky terrain. The bulk of Greece's crops are grown in the eastern Grecian plains of Thessaly, Macedonia, and Thrace. And that's exactly where I found myself as I slowly made my way toward Turkey. In an unending pattern for two solid days, dun-colored fields of cereal grains were on my right and hillside farms growing olives, grapes, melons, and tomatoes were on my left. Wheat fields in Greece are smaller than those in the plains of America—eastern Montana, the Dakotas, Nebraska, and Kansas—but they were good size nonetheless. When I left on my trip, I had missed wheat harvest in Kansas. I did not miss it in Greece.

After escaping the gay truck driver and following a short night's rest in the field, I couldn't wait to get on the road again. About the only vehicles coming by, however, or at least the only ones that wanted to stop, were combines. The combines were just like those at home, a few years older perhaps, but capable of harvesting ripened wheat for hours on end. I rode three or four combines that day, an agonizingly slow way to make it across the vast open plains of eastern Greece.

I rode a combine until it had to pull over and work its assigned field, then I'd catch another one—and so it went throughout the day, unbearably slow and painfully monotonous. At day's end, after traveling almost fifty miles, both tired and hungry, I gave up. Naturally, I chose a harvested wheat field as my bed for the night, full of hope that the next day would be much better.

Traffic was sparse as I spent an uncomfortable night in the wheat field and it didn't improve much in the early morning hours the next day. For the second consecutive day, I found myself riding more combines. After just a few miles, I got fed up with our tortoise-like progress, and asked the driver to let me off. He did—in the middle of nowhere: no houses, no towns, nothing in sight but unending fields of wheat. With the paucity of traffic, I might have guessed I was getting close to the Turkish border, but at the time the thought didn't cross my mind. I waited another three-and-a-half hours in that desolate spot until a driver took me the final sixty miles to Turkey. In the two days since I left Athens, I never saw a tourist, a tourist bus, or another hitchhiker.

I spent five days and nights in Greece, far longer than I spent in other countries. Not as long as the nine-plus day voyage on the *Tide* across the Atlantic, but five times as long as I had spent in France or England and ten times as long as I had spent in Belgium and Luxembourg. Of the five nights in Greece, only one night was spent in a hotel and I took only one shower. No wonder I was having trouble catching rides! The three days with the English nurses had been enjoyable, but the two days in Greece without them had been long, tiring, and exasperating. I was more than ready to say goodbye to Greece.

Turkey, Syria, and into Jordan

Turkey is a rectangle-shaped country about a thousand miles from east to west and half that distance from north to south. The northern part borders the Black Sea between Bulgaria and Georgia, and the southern portion edges the Aegean and Mediterranean Seas between Greece and Syria. The country is unique in that the western third is in Europe and the eastern two thirds are part of Asia. Its large, semi-arid central plateau is rimmed by hills and mountains, the highest and most famous of which is Mount Ararat, the supposed final resting place of Noah's Ark.

Historic battle sites from antiquity to modern times are found in almost every sector of Turkey. One memorable event, if you believe it was an historical event rather than a myth, took place in Troy in the 13th or 12th century BC. After a ten-year siege, the Achaeans used the ploy of a wooden horse with soldiers concealed inside to get within the walls of Troy and consequently defeat the Trojans. Turkey's long history abounds with similar stories. I didn't go to old Troy or other seaport towns, except Istanbul. In fact, I spent relatively little time in a country so large and with so much to offer. I went through Turkey almost as quickly as I had gone through the much smaller countries of Belgium, Luxembourg, and Switzerland. I also violated one of my own tenets of travel: in Turkey, I traveled a whole lot during nighttime.

The American Embassy personnel in Athens had been truthful; I had no trouble passing through immigration and customs when I crossed into Turkey. As soon as I crossed the border, I caught a quick and fast ride. Or perhaps I just thought the ride was fast after riding a half-dozen combines in Greece the previous two days. Nonetheless, from the Grecian-Turkish border the road goes straight to the city of Istanbul and I got there with a single ride. Much of the ride through western Turkey was across wide open and desolate-looking country, similar to the southwest part of the US, minus the sagebrush, thistles, and saguaro cactus.

Despite the excellent ride to Istanbul, the driver let me off just before sunset only fifteen or twenty blocks inside the city limits. That's when I first heard it: Arabic sounds over a loudspeaker, apparently shouting out instructions. (Over the next six weeks, I would hear the same sound seemingly a million times.) The sound was the *azan*—the Islamic call to prayer. For some Muslims, the obligatory call is scheduled at five periods of the day—near dawn, after midday has passed and the sun starts downwards, in the afternoon, just after sunset, and around nightfall. Under some circumstances, the ritual is shortened or combined, particularly the sunset and nightfall calls, but five times a day is most common throughout most of the Islamic world.

The call to prayer is issued from a *muezzin*, the chosen person at each mosque who leads and recites the call for every event of prayer and worship for the mosque. In former times, the muezzin called out personally from the top of a minaret at one corner of the mosque, but in modern times, a loudspeaker positioned in a minaret is used, particularly in large cities. And Istanbul is a large city: the largest city in Europe at thirteen million people and the third largest Islamic city in the world behind Jakarta, Indonesia and Cairo, Egypt.

Leaving me stranded near the far western edge of the city left me little choice. So I did what I always do when I'm in a major city: I took a taxi as far as possible. In this case, "as far as possible" just happened to be to the Bosporus Strait, also known as the Istanbul Strait or Dardanelle Straits, commonly called the "Dardanelles." Regardless of the name, I needed to cross the stretch of water that connects the Sea of Marmara (and ultimately the Black Sea) to the Aegean Sea (and ultimately the Mediterranean Sea.) It is this exact location that clearly defines the separation between the two continents of Europe and Asia.

The English-speaking taxi driver provided a real favor; he took me directly to the ferry that transported people and their vehicles to the Asian side of Turkey. Without attracting notice, I jumped into the back of a truck onboard the ferry, hoping to catch a long ride once we landed on the eastern shore. My plan didn't work out. The driver evidently saw me in the back of his truck, took me only five miles, and then asked me to get out. Conveniently, however, we stopped at a truck stop, so I was able to eat and drink and wash up a little. There, at a truck stop, I touched down on my third continent, almost as far west as a person can get in Asia. Little did I know then that within three years I would get to know a country in eastern Asia much better—South Vietnam.

It was well after dark and it would have been easy to find a corner somewhere to sleep until morning, but I wasn't sleepy, so I decided to go on. I asked a few truckers for a ride but was turned down several times in the course of two or three hours. The last driver and passenger I asked also turned me down, but as they slowly drove away from the gas pump, I stupidly threw my suitcase into the back of the truck and jumped on after it. (I almost didn't catch the truck and vowed to never do that again!) Neither the driver nor the passenger saw me or heard me climb aboard. I was thrilled with my deceptive scheme and my good fortune. I had the entire back of the truck to myself and the truck was full of comfortable canvasses and tarps for me to lie on. However, my good luck didn't last long. No more than five or six miles down the road, the driver pulled over and the passenger got out and climbed into the back of the truck with me. On a moonless night without nearby lights, the passenger didn't see me. He also didn't see my suitcase which I had covered with a tarp so the driver couldn't see it through the rearview mirror. The passenger made himself comfortable and quickly went to sleep. In the quiet stillness of the Turkish night without traffic going by, I was certain he could hear my breathing or my heartbeat, but apparently he didn't, and we spent the night no more than eight or ten feet apart.

The man in the back of the truck woke up before I did and I'm sure he was scared when he saw me. I sure know he terrified me when I awoke and saw him standing over me. I've never taken a single lesson of Arabic, but I'm sure he yelled, "Get the hell out of my truck, right now!"—or words to that effect. I grabbed my suitcase and bounced over the side of the truck and high-tailed it along the road heading east. About two minutes later, the truck passed by me and both the driver and passenger yelled at me, shook their fists, and otherwise made lewd gestures in sign language. I vowed to ask permission the next time I hopped in the back of someone's truck.

Once the two angry guys passed me, I waited a while for my first ride of the day. While standing there, I realized it was the 4th of July. That date has no special meaning in Turkey, but it certainly does in the US. I started to think about what I'd miss back home. My family would gather for a picnic with hotdogs, hamburgers, and chips, topped off with watermelon, but more relevantly, fireworks would help celebrate our Independence Day. Mom's side of the family was always much more into fireworks than dad's. With mom having eleven brothers and sisters (and three more who died in infancy), her family was exceedingly poor as one might imagine. Nonetheless, her family always scrounged up some money somewhere for fireworks, much to the delight of us grandkids. City law allowed us to shoot off fireworks within the city limits, so we did just that, right in grandma and grandpa's front yard and in the dirt street in front of their house. To top it off, they lived only three blocks from the county fairgrounds where every year the city had their own fireworks display. The whole family sat on the porch for a virtual front-row seat for the colorful, noisy spectacle. Well, there were no fireworks for me this year. I missed my paternal grandparent's fiftieth wedding anniversary the previous month and now I missed the traditional 4th of July celebration. I wondered what other big events back home I might miss this summer.

I was shaken from my 4th of July reverie as a car stopped and gave me a ride for 50 miles. That ride was soon followed by the single longest ride of my entire trip. I rode in the back of an American-made pickup truck for more than 400 miles. The driver even took me through Turkey's capital city, Ankara. In every country I visited, I had been in or through the capital city. (That held true for the entire trip with two exceptions—Morocco's capital city of Rabat and Canada's capital city of Ottawa.) As soon as the pickup driver dropped me off, I flagged down a bus and rode for free for seventy miles. When the bus reached its destination for the night, I walked a half-mile outside of town and slept in a field for the rest of the night. There wasn't much night left since it was after 2:00 a.m. I had been on the road for twenty-one hours straight and had probably waited no more than forty-five minutes for rides the entire day. That good fortune notwithstanding, it was an uneventful and quite forgettable 4th of July.

After resting to well past sun-up, I walked back into town to grab a bite to eat and wash up. While there, I noticed passengers getting on the same bus I had ridden the day before. The bus was bound for Adana, Turkey, 200 miles south and the last major town in Turkey before the Syrian border. I hopped aboard the bus.

In the early weeks of my trip, I wasn't observant of peoples' dress. But in Turkey, I noticed a lot of men wearing exceedingly baggy pants. A tradition carried over from both the Persian Empire and later the Ottoman Empire, many Turkish men wear pants loose at the hips and crotch and tight at the knees or ankles. Called Ottoman salvar pants, the pants are made of satin, silk, or light cotton and easily have enough room in the crotch for the testicles of three bull elephants. From the knee down, however, the pant legs are like ordinary trousers. Some Turkish women also wear salvar pants but their trousers were always covered by a salvar kameez or standard shirt normally with elaborate embroidery and embellishment. Due to the women's colorful shirts and lengthy scarves, salvar pants on women were less noticeable. Still, when Turkish men wore standard western shirts and salvar trousers, I found the combination amusing.

I made such good progress in Turkey that once the bus stopped in Adana, I slowed down and enjoyed a leisurely afternoon in town. I ate a good meal and drank several ice-cold Cokes. As I traveled east, I noticed drinks with ice were more and more rare. In the coming weeks, I was to find out that not only was ice rare, it was non-existent in many places in the Middle East and North Africa. I took the time to write two long letters home, and then unhurriedly made my way to the edge of town.

No major highway or thoroughfare covers the 220 miles between Adana, Turkey and Aleppo, Syria—the next major city on my route to the Holy Land. By 7:00 p.m., however, I had covered enough ground to find myself on foot once again, about six or seven miles north of the Syrian border. Unlike the difficulty I had traveling the final few miles in Greece, as I approached the Turkish border, I waited only a few minutes before getting a ride into Syria. Again, without ordeal, I exited Turkey and entered Syria, having no trouble at either side of the border with either customs or immigration.

Fortune smiled on me once more when I met two English-speaking Turkish students driving to Aleppo. Even as day turned to night, I saw the desolate, mountainous desert terrain and the absence of houses and towns. Traffic was sparse in either direction, with only a car or two passing every fifteen or twenty minutes. I saw no trucks. As we expeditiously made it toward Aleppo, I felt lucky to have escaped that bleak and isolated terrain, even though the students charged me $1.40 for the ride. That amount was not exorbitant, but was three or four times the amount for a bus ride—if a bus had been going in that direction.

Once we arrived in Aleppo, we decided to share a hotel room—if we could call it that. The hotel desk clerk cashed one of my remaining twenty-dollar traveler's checks and I paid my third of the room rate—forty-six cents. We climbed the dilapidated stairs to the second floor and entered a corner room not only without a lock, but without a door knob. The room was large with three single beds— more like Army cots really—in the center of the room spaced about three feet apart. Each bed had a bottom sheet, but no top sheet or pillow. The room was absent of furniture, pictures, or closets of any kind. Despite these shortcomings, the most noticeable aspect of the entire room was the windows. Windows, in this case, was a misnomer. Actually, they were window openings, completely absent of either glass or screens. Each opening was four or five feet across and six or seven feet high. We were on the second floor, but anyone with a decent-sized ladder could make their way into the room without the slightest struggle.

As Spartan as the sleeping quarters were, they were the hotel's best asset. The bathroom had a single shower stall (without a shower curtain) and in lieu of a shower spigot, a rusty half-inch pipe protruded from the shower wall six feet above the floor. The shower head had been removed decades ago and there was no hot water. The most sordid aspect of the bathroom, however, was the sink. A single spigot drained directly onto the floor. It looked as if someone had taken a sledge hammer and knocked out the bottom or bowl of the sink, leaving jagged, razor sharp porcelain edges on all sides of the opening. Once the water hit the floor, it slowly but conveniently meandered its way over to the shower drain. No soap was available for either the shower or sink. In addition, the whole room stunk horribly, but the toilet functioned perfectly and even toilet paper was provided. At one time, sixty or eighty years earlier, this hotel must have been grand. But now, at forty-six cents a night per person, surely we overpaid.

I hid my suitcase as well as I could, not from my two roommates, but from intruders that might come through the unlocked door or the window openings. Putting off a shower until morning, I crashed into the bed, the first one I'd seen since Athens.

Despite the traffic noise outside, I slept late thanks to the combination of fatigue and the comfort of the bed, a welcome change from the cold, hard ground I had grown used to. Once I took my first shower in a week, I changed into fresh clothes, left the hotel, and caught a southbound city bus to the edge of town. I focused on getting to Damascus, the capital of Syria and the country's second largest city.

A short ride took me twenty-five miles outside Aleppo and then I was picked up once again by two friendly college students. Both were fluent in English and Arabic and we enjoyed each other's company. From Aleppo to Damascus we spent over ten hours traveling together. They bought me a number of drinks for which I was truly grateful. Unfortunately, the students were not going all the way to Damascus. They were taking a cutoff about forty miles north of Damascus and were heading south-east and then east into Baghdad, Iraq. They offered me a ride there, but I declined, saying that getting to the Holy Land was much more important for me. Perhaps I could travel to Baghdad another time. (I never did go to Iraq, but as an Army Ranger, my son spent several months there nearly forty years later.) My last ride into Damascus was with a black Syrian and we shared a hotel room for fifty cents apiece. The room was ten times the quality of the room where I stayed in Aleppo the night before.

Some scholars say Damascus is the oldest continually inhabited city in the world, dating back to at least the second millennium BC. The city is also a major cultural and religious center of the Levant—a geographic and cultural term referring to the eastern Mediterranean region including most of modern Lebanon, Syria, Jordan, Palestine, Israel, and parts of southern Turkey. After my second shower in two days, I walked to a Muslim mosque to satisfy my curiosity.

The major mosque in Damascus, the Umayyad Mosque, is not an ordinary Muslim mosque. As a Levant icon for centuries, the Umayyad Mosque, is also known as the Great Mosque of Damascus. It remains one of the largest and oldest mosques in the world and is the fourth-holiest place in the Islamic world.

As required, I took off my shoes when I entered. Since mosques are places of worship, loud talking or discussion of topics deemed disrespectful is forbidden where people are praying. I couldn't go all the way inside, but got close enough to observe scores of men bowing in prayer. Islamic law does not mandate men and women be separated in the prayer hall, but traditional rules have segregated them. Often women are told to occupy the rows behind the men. That day, I saw no women in the mosque, either alongside the men or behind them.

After fifteen minutes at the mosque, I returned to the hotel to pick up my suitcase. The clerk advised me which bus to take out of town, and I was soon heading for Jordan and the Holy Land. It's a short 110 miles from Damascus to Amman, the capital and principal city of Jordan. The border of Jordan was half that distance and I made it with ease in less than an hour.

Because the distances between major towns were great in Turkey and Syria, I sped through the two countries much more quickly than in other countries. I also spent only two nights in hotels in Turkey and Syria combined. Except for my encounter with a fellow sleeper in the back of a truck, and for the deplorable conditions of an Aleppo hotel room, my stay in other countries would be far more eventful.

The Holy Land

Three major world religions—Judaism, Islam, and Christianity—consider the Holy Land and its historic religious sites spiritually meaningful. The exact boundaries of the Holy Land are not clearly defined as borders between nations or states, and each of the three religions offer different interpretations of the geographical range covered by the term "Holy Land."

For Judaism, the Holy Land refers to the Land of Israel based on the religious significance of Jerusalem, the holiest city to Judaism. The Holy Land of Israel is generally implied in the Torah—the Jewish holy book containing the five books of Moses—Genesis, Exodus, Leviticus, Numbers, and Deuteronomy. Israelites feel God gave them the land and it is the "promised land," an integral part of God's covenant. Four Israeli cities — Jerusalem, Hebron, Tzfat, and Tiberias—are considered Judaism's holiest cities. Jerusalem is mentioned 669 times in the Hebrew Bible and the "Land of Israel" appears 154 times.

In the Islamic holy book the Koran, the term "Holy Land" is mentioned at least seven times, once when Moses proclaims to the children of Israel, "O my people! Enter the holy land which Allah hath assigned unto you, and turn not back ignominiously, for then will ye be overthrown, to your own ruin." For Muslims, the exact region of the Holy Land, referred to as "Blessed Land" in Koran verse 21:71, has been interpreted differently by various scholars. Some say it is a wide range of land which includes Syria, Palestine, and the cities of Tyre and Sidon. Others say it includes Damascus, Palestine, and a small part of Jordan. Still other Islamic followers firmly believe the Holy Land to be the Levant, the entire eastern Mediterranean Sea area.

For Christians (and many Muslims), the Holy Land refers to the area between the Jordan River and the Mediterranean Sea, the assumed place of Jesus's ministry. Christians consider the land of Israel and parts of Jordan holy because of its association with the birth, ministry, crucifixion, and resurrection of Jesus of Nazareth whom they regard as the Savior or Messiah. The perceived holiness of the land to Christianity was a motivational factor behind the efforts of the Crusades, which sought to win the Holy Land back from the Muslim Turks, who had conquered it from the Muslim Arabs, who had in turn conquered it from the Christian Byzantine Empire. Strange as it may seem, outside of the places traditionally associated with Christian personalities, the Holy Land bears no special mention in the Christian Bible.

Regardless of its ill-defined boundaries, Jews, Muslims, and Christians have made pilgrimages to religious sites in the Holy Land since biblical times. Most people visit the Holy Land to touch and see physical manifestations of their faith, to confirm their beliefs in the holy context, and to personally connect to the Holy Land itself. Professor of Jewish Philosophy at The Hebrew University of Jerusalem, Eliezer Schweid states, "The uniqueness of the Land of Israel is "geo-theological ... This is the land which faces the entrance of the spiritual world...beyond the physical world known to us through our senses,"

Like millions before me, I entered the Holy Land with enthusiasm and excitement. And despite what others say, in my view, in 1965, the Holy Land consisted of only two nations—Israel and Jordan. Israel was inarguable. And Bethlehem, the birthplace of Jesus, was in Jordan. Besides, don't the national boundary lines of Jordan form the shape of an angel? How could it be anything but Holy Land? (In December, 1995, under the *Interim Agreement on the West Bank and Gaza Strip*, Bethlehem was ceded to Palestine and remains under control of that nation today.) As I crossed into Jordan, I vowed to slow down and allow myself enough time to see and fully experience the holiest of sites, particularly those associated with the birth, crucifixion, and resurrection of Christ.

I crossed the Syrian-Jordanian border without incident and quickly caught a short ride to Amman. Since I was dropped off downtown, I found the main bus station and took a bus from Amman to Jerusalem. The landscape between Amman and Jerusalem can only be described as the most God-forsaken land I've ever seen—nothing but hills and rocks and completely absent of arable farmland of any kind. If this land was the "Promised Land" described in the Old Testament, I was evidently missing something or God hadn't yet seen the fertile farmlands of Iowa, Indiana, Illinois, or California's productive San Joaquin valley. My first impression of the Promised Land was that it looked like a desert and stood in stark contrast to the green farm fields of France, the lush, grassy meadows of Switzerland, or the golden fields of wheat in eastern Greece. Perhaps this terrain was an aberration; I would keep my eyes and my mind open.

The bus stopped in Jerusalem at the outer edge of the city, not in the city center where main bus stations are normally found. I didn't think much of it at the time since my goal was to catch another bus to Bethlehem. My plan was to stay or live in Bethlehem for a about a week and then go into Jerusalem as often as I wanted or needed to visit the sites I traveled so far to see.

It's a short six miles from Jerusalem to Bethlehem and I arrived by bus in the city of Jesus's birth at 7:00 p.m. on July 7th . I found an excellent hotel no more than 200 feet from Jesus's birthplace with the added convenience of the Bethlehem post office half that distance in the other direction. I paid $6.00 for the hotel room—not for one night, but for five nights. I was delighted because both the price and the quality of the room were the best I'd seen since I left Rome. I bought a cheap meal and a Coke at a nearby café, took a long, hot shower, and wrote some letters home. Before I went to bed that night, I wrote in my diary, "Mentally and emotionally, I feel better today than on any other day since I left." I had made it; I was finally in the Holy Land!

Comfortable in a decent bed for the first time in what seemed like ages, I slept late and leisurely took my time to eat a decent breakfast and mail the letters I wrote the night before. My intention was to enjoy a relaxing, unhurried first day in the Holy Land without scheduling or visiting holy sites either in Bethlehem or Jerusalem.

With a day of relaxation or leisure in mind, I stumbled onto (or into) the local pool hall. Two dozen boys my age or younger were crowded around four old and worn-out pool tables. On each table, the cloth was as threadbare as a pair of ten-year-old jeans and on two tables, there were spots where the cloth was missing entirely and the slate was fully exposed. I observed that none of the tables were completely level, which forced everyone to shoot much harder than necessary just to keep their shots online. Despite the shabby condition of the tables, everyone seemed to be having a good time, so I joined right in.

All of the boys were Muslims or Christians and all were friendly and outgoing. Even though their native language was Arabic, when they spoke to me, they used English. Some of them spoke English well and I soon felt as comfortable around them as if I were around friends in my hometown pool hall in Garden City. During the course of a dozen games or so, I let my new friends know I had just arrived the night before and had not seen anything yet. With unbridled pride in their home town, two boys insisted that after they went home for lunch, they would meet me at my hotel and personally take me inside the Church of the Nativity.

The Church of the Nativity is considered to be the oldest continuously operating Christian church in the world. Constantine and his mother Helena originally commissioned the church in AD 327 over the cave site still considered to be the birthplace of Jesus. The original basilica was completed in AD 339 but fire destroyed it in the sixth century. The Byzantine Empire built a new basilica in AD 565, restoring the architectural tone of the original. As discomforting as it may be to Protestants and Catholics, the birthplace of Jesus is under a Greek Orthodox Church. Catholics may be reassured to know, however, a Catholic church adjoins the Greek Orthodox one.

To get into the church, the two boys and I entered through a low door no more than three feet high, called the "Door of Humility." The church features golden mosaics covering the side walls and a complex array of lamps throughout the entire building. Stairways on either side of the Sanctuary led us down to the cave below. Below an altar, a fourteen-pointed silver star set into the marble floor marks the exact spot of Jesus's birth. Although the altar is supposedly denominationally neutral, two solemn-looking bearded Greek Orthodox priests guarded the site. Or perhaps they were guarding the offerings. Money of every denomination, both paper and coins, lay directly on the floor near the star. I recognized American dollars, French francs, Italian lire, and Greek drachmas, but there must have been money there from fifty or sixty other nations. Except for the earthly aspect of the money, the entire setting was both emotionally and spiritually moving. My two friends and I spent ten reflective minutes in silent prayer in perhaps the most serene and tranquil place I had ever been. While there, I never felt more humble or closer to God.

The boys then took me to another part of the church where they showed me the skeletal remains of boys under two years old supposedly executed by Herod the Great. The story, as related in the Gospel of Matthew verses 2:16-18, is commonly known in Christian history as the "Massacre of the Innocents."

Visiting the Church of the Nativity left me more spiritually aware than I had ever been previously. I said goodbye to the boys and returned to my hotel room only a few feet away. Near sunset, I stepped out for an evening meal and then returned early still touched by the afternoon's venture. Then, I did something I hadn't done for many years; I started reading the Bible. One was conveniently placed in the hotel room's bedside table, along with an Arabic version of the Koran. I began with the New Testament but before I read the first word, I promised myself to go to the Holy City of Jerusalem the next day and walk where Jesus had trod almost two thousand years earlier.

I slept later than usual and after grabbing some unleavened bread and a Coke, I caught a bus to Jerusalem. I was excited about the wonderful things I might see that day and also excited about entering another country—Israel. Before the day was over, I saw several spiritually moving sites, but I didn't get into Israel, not on this trip anyway.

In 1965, Jerusalem was a divided city. Over the centuries, hundreds of battles and wars have been fought and many nations have ruled the city. For nineteen years, however, two countries—Israel and Jordan—were forced to share it. In November 1947, the United Nations decided to partition Palestine into two states, one Jewish and one Arab. The Arabs disagreed with the new borders and began rioting. When Israel was declared a nation in May, 1948, the fighting intensified. Six months later, the military leaders of the two nations decided upon an international border inside Jerusalem and an ugly concrete wall was built segregating the city. Both sides thought this agreement would be short lived and many hoped the temporary division would lead to a peace treaty and permanent borders. Permanent borders—if one believes borders are ever permanent—were realized only at the end of the Arab-Israeli War (often called the Six-Day War) in June 1967.

I arrived in Jerusalem but was not allowed to cross into the Jewish or Israeli part of the city. At that time, except for political and religious officials, non-Jewish people were denied access from an Arabic country directly into Israel. If I wanted to go to Israel, I needed to return to Greece or Cyprus or another non-Arab nation and go to Israel by plane or boat. With virtually no money, none of those were good options for me. Fortunately, the holy sites associated with the crucifixion, death, and resurrection of Christ were in the Christian quarter of the city (the Jordanian side) and that's exactly where I arrived a little after 11:00 a.m.

Fair or unfair, my first impression of Jerusalem was the city was filthy with grime built up from two or three millennia. Sanitation in ancient Middle Eastern cities and sanitation in modern American cities is not the same. In some areas of Jerusalem, the smell was horrific. I noticed small butcher shops in other Arabic cities with freshly cut meat, mostly chicken and lamb, hanging from hooks, completely unwrapped. But in Jerusalem, there were more shops and they all appeared much dirtier. Flies and other insects were common. I suppose once fresh meat is cooked or boiled, having had flies on it the last several hours might not affect its quality or taste, but it sure looked disgusting. For those who didn't want their chickens killed and plucked, live chickens in homemade reed baskets were an arm's length away from the freshly cut meat. Stepping inside a couple of small grocery stores—the mid-sixties equivalent of our modern "7-11", I noticed several items were sold in small amounts. Salt, sugar, pepper, olives, raisins, and a variety of other commodities were sold in any amount from open cloth sacks. If shoppers needed a teaspoon of salt or two tablespoons of sugar, they simply bought the amount they needed without getting a five or ten-pound bag of the item. Just as the freshly cut meat was uncovered, so too were these other groceries. But I didn't come ten thousand miles to Jerusalem to buy meat or sugar; I was looking for the footsteps of Jesus.

In the maze of Jerusalem's back streets and alleyways, it took me a while to find it, but finally I saw and entered the Church of the Holy Sepulchre. The church is constructed over the site recognized as Mount Calvary, where Jesus was crucified, and also contains the place where Jesus was buried—the Sepulchre. The exact location of Mount Calvary comes solely from its identification by Helena, the mother of Constantine I, in AD 325. Helena also identified the location of the tomb of Jesus and claimed to have discovered the actual cross itself. Her son Constantine then built the Church of the Holy Sepulchre around the entire site.

The Church of the Holy Sepulchre is also known by some Christians as the Church of the Resurrection, the purported site of the resurrection of Jesus. For many Christians, this site remains the most important pilgrimage destination since the fourth century, and arguably the holiest site in all Christendom. Even so, some regard the alternative Garden Tomb, elsewhere in Jerusalem, as the true place of Jesus's crucifixion and resurrection.

Controversy aside, the Church of the Holy Sepulchre houses an inlaid stone disc about three or four feet in diameter, where supposedly the cross of Jesus once stood. I lined up with other visitors to see and to marvel at the exact spot and to touch the rock of Calvary in the Chapel of Crucifixion. The church also houses the Stone of Unction, also known as the Stone of Anointing. The Stone is a polished tan and red and measures about a yard wide and fifteen or sixteen feet long. The Stone is significant in that it's supposedly the place where the body of Jesus was laid down after being removed from the cross. As customary at the time, Jesus was anointed and wrapped in shrouds in preparation for burial. I was humbled, inspired, and full of reverence as I knelt and touched the Stone.

After an hour in the Church of the Holy Sepulchre, I walked to the St. Peter in Gallincantu Church where allegedly Peter denied Jesus and heard the cock crow three times. This church is also over the site of the prison room where Jesus spent his last night before his crucifixion. The "hole" is not a room or a prison cell in the traditional sense, but an extremely large cistern with a large opening at the top. I made my way to the bottom of the cistern via a narrow, circular stairway. In Jesus's day, the only way in which a prisoner was added or removed was by ropes from above. That method for Jesus's removal is depicted in a mosaic on an outside wall of the church.

The path Jesus walked from the prison to Mount Calvary is called the Via Dolorosa or Way of Grief or Painful Way. The route has fourteen stations of which the last five are located inside the Church of the Holy Sepulcher where I had been less than an hour before. The current route, established since the 18th century, winds crookedly some 600 to 700 yards between the two churches. As I walked along the path and I stopped at each of the nine outside stations, I couldn't help but think of the scene from the movie *Ben Hur* in which the shadow of the cross of Jesus cures Ben Hur's mother and sister of leprosy. Perhaps I should have thought of other things, perhaps other miracles of Jesus, but I was simply caught up in the joy and sense of accomplishment I felt at walking in his footsteps.

By mid-afternoon, I made my way to two more churches, the first of which was the Church of the Sepulchre of Saint Mary, also known as the Tomb of the Virgin Mary, at the foot of the Mount of Olives. Eastern Orthodox Christians believe this site to be the burial place of Mary, the mother of Jesus. Lastly, I made my way to the Chapel of the Ascension, a shrine located on the Mount of Olives, believed to be the earthly spot where Jesus ascended into Heaven forty days after his resurrection. The Chapel of the Ascension is part of a larger complex consisting of a Christian church, a monastery, and an Islamic mosque. According to the faithful, the Chapel houses a slab of stone believed to contain one of Jesus's footprints.

By late afternoon, I returned to Bethlehem by bus. I had an early evening meal, wrote letters to tell the people back home what I had seen and experienced, and continued reading the New Testament.

For the next two or three days, nothing eventful happened and I fell into a boring routine. I enjoyed the comfort and quality of my hotel room, so I slept late, had a late breakfast, played pool for two or three hours, checked the post office for letters both in Bethlehem and Jerusalem, and read the Bible. Since I was getting low on funds, I made no other pilgrimages to holy sites, even though I wanted to go to city of Nazareth and the resort at the Dead Sea. For the first time, I got really homesick.

Not because I had been gone away from home for nearly seven weeks, but because I had extra time on my hands. Hitchhiking the 2,700 miles from London to the Holy Land as quickly as I did didn't allow me the time to get homesick. Now, things were different. I had more time to think of home. Whenever I was feeling melancholy, however, I went to the Church of the Nativity next door and always felt much better when I returned.

Something else was on my mind. I needed to get to Egypt. I didn't have the money to fly (from Amman) and I didn't want to walk across the Sinai Desert the way Moses and his people did during the Exodus more than three thousand years before. That left me two routes— two water routes to be exact. The first was to go to Beirut, Lebanon and take a ship to Egypt from there. The second choice was to hitchhike to Aqaba, Jordan and catch a ship sailing through the Red Sea to the Indian Ocean and back up the Suez Canal to Egypt. An important decision had to be made but I would think about it the next day. Today, I had more important things to think about; tonight was my last night in the hotel.

I paid for five nights at the hotel and wasn't sure how much longer I would or could stay in Bethlehem. While I contemplated my options, I marched to the pool hall to spend a couple of hours. On that day, I met a senior in high school named Victor Batarseh and we quickly became friends. His father owned a local construction company and they had a big house. He was the youngest of five children and two of his siblings, both adults, were currently living in America, so they had plenty of room for me in their home. When we parted, Victor said he'd go home and ask his parents if I could stay with them a while. I returned to the hotel, retrieved my suitcase, and waited in lobby for Victor to return. He didn't come. Seeing me resting uncomfortably in a chair in the lobby, the hotel clerk took pity on me and let me back into my room for the night. He told me to get up early the next morning and be out of the room before the day manager arrived. Getting an extra night in a hotel room for free was an unexpected surprise and waking up early was never a problem.

I was up and out of the hotel at 5:30 a.m. sitting in a nearby café when Victor spotted me there two hours later. Immediately, he took me home to meet his parents and they not only offered me a nice breakfast, but invited me to stay with them a few days. I had hit the jackpot! What a wonderful gesture on their part. At least for a few days, I would have a roof over my head and a place to eat, and I could procrastinate on the decision of how to get to Egypt.

The Batarsehs were a Christian family consisting of the mother (Marie) and father (William) and five children. Their only daughter, an adult, was a Catholic nun assigned to a church in America. Their oldest son William still lived at home and was studying locally to become a Catholic priest. Another adult son was studying in Atlanta, Georgia to be a Protestant minister. Proudly displayed on the fireplace mantel was a photograph of their second son with the Reverend Billy Graham's arm around his shoulders. Two teenage sons remained at home, Tony and Victor, and both thought they would someday follow in their big brothers' footsteps.

After breakfast, Victor and I played several games of pool, I returned to the hotel lobby to fetch my suitcase, and I moved in with the Batarsehs early in the afternoon. Mr. Batarseh and I discussed the possibility of me doing construction work for $1.15 a day. I was to visit the construction site in a day or two. After supper, Victor and I played chess until 3:00 a.m.

The next day, Wednesday, July 14th, I finally received my first letter from home. Dad had written a long letter and naturally, I was overjoyed to get it. The letter was the first contact with anyone from home since I called him by phone from New York. By afternoon, I had the letter memorized. I didn't know it at the time, but Loretta had sent three or four letters to Bethlehem. Unfortunately, she addressed them to Bethlehem, Israel, not Bethlehem, Jordan. Consequently, all the letters were returned to her and I didn't get a letter from her until I reached Madrid. That night, Victor and I saw two American movies, one with Brigitte Bardot and one with Alan Ladd, but the names of the movies elude me.

Victor and I slept late. Early in the afternoon, Mr. Batarseh took us to his current construction site. The work methods appeared crude with a heavy dose of manual labor and a real absence of mechanical and electrical tools. I was told the top wage earner makes $7.50 a day, but a person who straightens nails all day makes one-tenth that amount. Seventy-five cents a day seemed like a terribly low wage, but then I remembered I did the same thing for my dad eight or nine years earlier for nothing. Mr. Batarseh did not offer me a job and I did not ask for one, so we went home and ate some of Tony's birthday cake. Later, William (the brother) and I went to the movie *Goldfinger*. I had a headache, a fever, and a stomach ache, so didn't enjoy the movie much. Could it have been the cake?

For the most part, the next three days in Bethlehem with the Batarsehs was uneventful. I still wasn't feeling well, so I wasn't motivated to do anything out of the ordinary. The boys and I played pool in the daytime and went to the movies in the evening, or stayed home and watched wrestling on TV. I tried to convince the Batarsehs the wrestling was fake, but they wouldn't believe me. Tony and I went to Jerusalem together and visited his aunt who lived there and checked with the Jerusalem post office one last time. No luck. When we returned, Ms. Batarseh cooked her best meal yet, in honor of relatives who had come to visit and my pending departure the next day. I felt much better by dinner time and thoroughly enjoyed the meal. They induced me to try a strong wine and I couldn't distinguish the flavor due to the strong alcohol content. After watching fake wrestling again for about five minutes, I said goodbye to the guests and went to my room where I finished reading the Gospel of Luke.

Over the course of the two previous days, I decided to try to get to Egypt by way of Aqaba. The decision, for the most part, was a financial one. I was told it cost $25 or $30 to go to Egypt by ship from Beirut, but if I caught a cargo ship in Aqaba, I might get to Egypt for virtually nothing. By mid-morning on Sunday, July 18th, I said goodbye to the Batarsehs and caught a bus to Amman. Mr. Batarseh gave me $5 and said it was just like giving money to a son. After taking me in off the street, their entire family treated me well and had epitomized not only the pinnacle of Christian hospitality, but the very essence of the Golden Rule. I vowed never to forget them (and I haven't) and to sometime in my life, help a stranger in need as I was in the summer of '65.

With the Batarseh's gracious generosity, I was able to spend twelve days in Bethlehem. True, I didn't visit all the holy sites in Bethlehem and Jerusalem, but I saw what was important to me. I fulfilled my personal goal of walking on the same path Jesus had walked during his last hours on earth, and been spiritually touched by the holy sites of his birth, crucifixion, death, and resurrection. Did the solemnity, reverence, and humility I experienced in these sites awaken in me a divine manifestation or epiphany? It was too early to tell. Meanwhile, I was nearly broke, 10,000 miles from home, and needed to find a way to get back.

Frustration in Aqaba

Late on Sunday morning, I caught a bus from Bethlehem to Amman. From the Amman bus station, I hired a taxi to take me to the only road to Aqaba. The distance from Amman to Aqaba on the Red Sea is 165 miles, almost due south across the barren desert terrain of the Nefud Desert. This was the same desert where British Army officer T.E. Lawrence nearly died of thirst while leading a troop of fifty Bedouins in a sneak attack upon the Turks. The seaport town of Aqaba was well-fortified against naval attack, but even the Bedouins wouldn't venture across the Nefud without the coercion of Lieutenant Lawrence. The attack was successful and a major turning point for the British during World War I in that part of the world. Forever after, Lieutenant Lawrence was known as "Lawrence of Arabia."

I missed Lawrence of Arabia by nearly five decades and my trip to Aqaba was much quicker and much more comfortable than his. Aqaba is Jordan's only coastal city and provides a seaway to connect the country to the Indian Ocean and the rest of the world. Almost all vehicular traffic leaving south from Amman was going to Aqaba—except for a side road to Petra. Petra is where the world-famous architecture was cut directly into stone in the fourth century BC and is modern Jordan's most visited tourist attraction. (The site plays a prominent role in the movie *Indiana Jones and the Last Crusade*.) I easily flagged down a truck and caught a ride going south.

Trucks in the Middle East are not the eighteen-wheeled semi-trucks ubiquitously found on interstate highways and turnpikes in America. Trucks in this part of the world and in North Africa as well, are more like large grain trucks—with two notable exceptions. Large grain trucks in the states have sides and end-gates about three feet high, and once fully loaded with wheat, corn, milo, soybeans, or other grains, they reach their weight capacity. In Jordan, "grain" trucks have extended sides and end-gates eight or ten feet above the truck bed. Often, goods are piled even higher than the sides. The trucks were a unique and comical sight; the fully loaded trucks look as high as they are long. The second clearly noticeable difference between these trucks and those found in America is the number and color of auxiliary lights. Auxiliary lights of every possible color adorn the cab, the sides, the frame, the bumpers, the mud flaps, and practically every other part of the truck. I'm convinced these trucks had more lights than the ceremonial Christmas tree at the White House!

Every truck I saw had at least one passenger or co-driver. That's where the real fun began for me. Not having to ride in the cab, I climbed to the top of whatever product the truck was hauling and sat high above and just behind the center of the cab. I removed my shirt and enjoyed the sun and sixty-miles-an-hour wind blowing through my hair. Leonardo DiCaprio had nothing on me when he stood on the bow of the *Titanic* in the 1997 movie of the same name and shouted, "I'm king of the world." I didn't yell that line, but over the coming weeks, I rode hundreds of miles high above the cabs of trucks and enjoyed every mile of it.

I say we sped along at sixty miles per hour, but that was on level roads without curves. Whenever we came upon a curve in the road, even the slightest curve, the driver was forced to slow down since the load was exceedingly top-heavy. On the sharpest of turns, even five miles an hour seemed dangerous. So even though the total distance from Amman to Aqaba was relatively short, it took several hours for heavily laden trucks to navigate the route.

Late in the afternoon, we stopped at a desert oasis where a far-sighted entrepreneur had constructed a primitive truck stop. I hopped down from my lofty perch and, along with the three men in the cab, went into a basic and rudimentary restaurant to get a good but inexpensive meal. We sat in homemade chairs at a square, rough-hewn table, without a tablecloth. The strangest thing about the meal was that instead of asking what each of us wanted to drink, the waitress put a one-pound Folgers coffee can full of room-temperature water right in the center of the table. As the meal progressed, I soon found out if I wanted a drink or needed to wash down the food, I must share that single can of water with the other three men at the table. And that's what I did.

Once we finished eating, the driver and passengers spent some time thoroughly checking over the truck, and I just coincidentally wandered toward an outside corner of the restaurant, There, I spotted our waitress getting another can of water from a four-foot-tall earthen pot with a sixteen or eighteen inch opening at the top. When she took the can into the restaurant, I sauntered over to the urn and took a look inside. The urn was positioned in a darkened corner, probably to keep

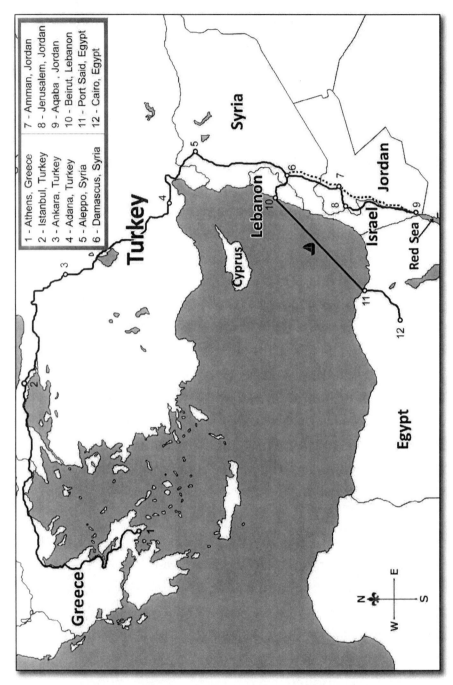

Athens, Greece to Cairo, Egypt

the water as cool as possible, and it was too dark to see if the water was clean or not. But in the water and clinging to the dampened side walls were about three or four dozen crickets. Not the dark black crickets commonly found in western Kansas, but brown-speckled crickets the same size as the black ones. This was many years before the popularity and easy availability of bottled water, and I left that restaurant more determined than ever to keep drinking Cokes or bottled drinks whenever I could.

We were at the truck stop for nearly two hours and by the time we got on the road again, it was after nightfall. That didn't dissuade me from reclaiming my elevated perch above the cab, but this time I had to wear a long-sleeved shirt and my college warm-up jacket too. We had driven only an hour when the driver pulled off the road where a couple of other trucks had done the same. Six or eight men were sitting around a small, makeshift campfire enjoying hot Turkish tea. The men at the campfire probably knew my three traveling companions so the latter were enthusiastically welcomed. A couple of men relaxed nearby smoking hashish from water pipes. No one seemed to have a care in the world.

The boiling hot tea was poured from a small and deeply blackened aluminum teapot into small tea glasses, about the size of standard whiskey shot glasses found in American bars. Instead of pouring the tea carefully from the pot to the glass, the man pouring the tea took great pride in raising the teapot high in the air and letting the scalding tea cascade into the glass he held carefully on the ground. Apparently, the higher the pour, the greater was his sense of accomplishment. The tea is strong enough that at least half the glass is filled with sugar. Even after adding sugar, I had to wait nearly ten minutes before I could put the glass to my lips.

My driver and his friends seemed to be in no hurry to move on, but a different truck left in an hour, so I caught a ride with the new driver. We finally arrived in Aqaba at 12:30 a.m. and I quickly walked a few blocks to the waterfront. When I arrived, three ships were in port and I was able to walk up to each one and ask where they were going once they left Aqaba. All three, including one American ship, were going east toward India and Southeast Asia. None were heading for the Suez Canal and Egypt. An hour and a half later, I found a truck stop and a corner to curl up in where I spent the rest of the night.

My next day started three hours later at 5:00 a.m. I awoke at the truck stop and walked into the main city to get some food. Unlike the night before, when I returned to the docks after breakfast, the gates were closed and carefully guarded. The guards wouldn't let me in to talk to the ships' personnel, so I went to three separate travel agencies before I found someone to vouch for me. When I returned to the docks, I showed the guards the personal note from the travel agency and the guards let me inside the locked gates. Again, I was able to approach three new ships. An American ship was bound for Bombay, India, so that option was out. A Greek ship was also going to India. A small Italian freighter was bound for Egypt, but they rudely refused me passage. I waited at the docks for a full six hours and, late in the afternoon, a German vessel arrived. I don't know if they were just messing with my mind or not, but they said I could go with them, but would have to go all the way to Bremen, Germany. I ruled that out. Near sundown, a Russian cargo ship pulled alongside the dock and I was able to board the ship and ask questions. I was impressed by the friendliness of the few Russian sailors I saw, but more impressed with their response. The ship was going to be in port for a few days and I was invited to come back the next day and talk directly to the captain. I left the waterfront and spent the night on the ground just outside the gate.

When the gate guard arrived for work at 7:00 a.m., he awoke me, and unlike the previous day, I encountered no problems getting through the gate and down to dockside. Four more ships arrived during the daytime, but none were heading for Egypt. My best shot appeared to be with the Russian ship, so I boarded her for the second time as she lay in anchor loading phosphate. This time, I met the captain personally, but he advised me to return at 1:00 or 2:00 p.m. the next day. I promised I would.

While I was standing and talking to the captain, an English-speaking Jordanian dock worker was telling some Russian sailors how he loved the Russians and hated Americans because of America's involvement in Vietnam. Whether he knew or cared I was within earshot didn't seem to matter; he continued to press his point. At that time, Vietnam meant nothing personally to me. That said, I'm almost certain it was the same Jordanian dock worker who the next day shouted at me, "Yankee, go home," the first time I had actually heard that expression. The expression was offensive enough in its own right, but I just happened to be standing next to a few dozen pallets of 100-pound bags of flour clearly marked, "Donated by the United States of America."

I hung around the docks for the second full day and a few more ships came in including the United States Navy's *USS Jonas Ingram*, a Forrest Sherman class destroyer. I made my way up the ship's gangway to talk to the officer in charge, but he quickly yet politefully informed me it was impossible for me to hitchhike aboard a US Navy vessel. Two more Italian cargo ships docked and both were going to Egypt through the Suez Canal. The thought crossed my mind to stow away on board an Italian ship, but that would have been virtually impossible to pull off, so with my suitcase in tow, I left the wharf and slept just outside the dock gates as I had the night before. As a lay there in the dark, I convinced myself the Russian ship was my only viable option. If the Russians wouldn't take me, I must resort to Plan B.

At 7:30 a.m., I walked a hundred yards and got a hotel room where I took my first shower since leaving the Batarsehs in Bethlehem four days earlier. With a fresh set of clothes and renewed optimism, I left my suitcase in the hotel and walked back to the dock. I wanted to try the last Italian ship one more time before finally giving up on them. I arrived late; the Italian ship had already left. There appeared nothing to do now but wait for the Russian ship to return to the phosphate berth and to try to convince the captain to allow me passage. The Russian ship wasn't scheduled to arrive until 1:00 p.m.

Since I had some extra time on my hands, I decided to go swimming in the Red Sea. I had brought a swimming suit along, but this was the first time I took the opportunity to use it. The Aqaba area is well-known in the Middle East for its white sandy beaches, but swimming is not the most popular attraction. The Red Sea near Aqaba is more famous for its warm water and rich marine life. A number of coral reefs just offshore attract hundreds of divers and snorkelers. I didn't dive or snorkel, but when I swam in the warm water, I felt remarkably refreshed and reinvigorated. Swimming in the Red Sea was the first time I had gone swimming in salt water and I found it much saltier than I imagined. The salt smell remained in my suit, in my hair, and on my skin. As I dried out in the sun, I wondered how many other places in the world a person could swim in one country and see two other countries from the same spot. Distant mountains in Saudi Arabia were on my left and nearby Egyptian mountains at the far eastern edge of the Sinai Desert were on my right.

Returning from the beach, I showered at the hotel and then boarded the Russian ship for the third time. The captain and other crew members were as gracious and friendly as they had been during the two previous visits. Apparently, the captain had some time on his hands and he asked me if I knew how to play chess. Although I had never been good at the game, I had recently played many games with Victor in Bethlehem. The captain and I played three or four games of chess in his personal living quarters until he tired of my ineptitude. He was hoping for a much better match. I was hoping for passage to Egypt. After offering me a bowl of what I can only describe as cold cabbage soup, he finally revealed he would not give me a ride to Egypt. Greatly disappointed, I left the Russian ship and walked away from the Aqaba dock for the last time.

During the three long days I had spent in Aqaba, I boarded nearly a dozen ships seeking passage to Egypt. Some of the people treated me kindly and politely; others were more forceful and terse; almost rude. The result, however, was the same: they all said no. There was nothing to do but swallow my pride and begin to execute my alternative plan—backtrack through Jordan and Syria and get to Beirut. I would try to book passage to Egypt from there.

After stopping by the hotel for another quick shower and to pick up my suitcase, I checked out and walked into town for an evening meal. By the time I finished eating, it was after 5:00 p.m., and I walked to the edge of town on the road leading to Amman. Waiting unsuccessfully for a ride for more than three hours, I cursed myself for checking out of the hotel too early. Yet,

I was too tired to walk all the way back to the hotel and too proud to ask for my room key back. It was well after 8:00 p.m. and nearly dark before I got my first ride heading north out of Aqaba—in a truck, of course.

I don't know if I was more frustrated in spending three, long fruitless days in Aqaba or having to retrace almost 300 miles back through Amman and Damascus. I had been to both of those places before, but with Israel dead smack in the way, retracing my steps through Jordan and Syria was the shortest and least expensive way to get to Beirut. Beirut was a seaport city located on the east end of the Mediterranean Sea, another seventy miles northwest of Damascus.

Unless you have experienced it, you can't believe how cold it gets in the desert at night. I was cold enough riding high in the back of the first truck from Aqaba that I voluntarily got off when the truck pulled over to add oil to the engine. That's the first time I had done that since I jumped off a combine in eastern Greece nearly three weeks before. I don't know the exact location, but it was somewhere north of the Petra cut-off, because when I got out, I met a husband and wife hitchhiking together, and they were headed for Petra. Those two people were the first hitchhikers I had seen since I left Athens. We had a short visit and wished each other luck, then headed in opposite directions.

It was after sun-up and much warmer when the second truck dropped me off in Amman. But I messed up somehow, took the wrong road out of town, and ended up in a small village at the end of a dead-end road. There was nothing to do but retrace my steps and go into the city of Amman—for the fourth time. And despite being in the city four times, I never took the time to see the cultural, religious, or historic sites. Even so, I felt I had spent a week there. By the time I returned to Amman and re-discovered the main highway to Damascus, I had wasted almost the entire day. Near sundown, I caught a ride to the Syrian-Jordanian border, cleared immigration and customs without incident on both sides of the border, and caught a taxi to take me from the border to Damascus. I told the taxi driver I had no money, but since he was taking another passenger anyway, he let me ride free. When we arrived, they both gave me some small Syrian coins which turned out to be almost fifty cents. I invested the money in some food since I hadn't eaten since 5:30 that morning.

After I left the small café in Damascus, two short car rides took me to the Syrian-Lebanese border. I paid $1.60 for a visa to enter the eleventh country on my trip—Lebanon. I had $48.50 to my name.

Trouble in Beirut

From the Syrian border, a fast-driving truck took me the short distance through the mountains and cedars of Lebanon to the city of Beirut. The driver took me all the way down to the dock where he needed to unload his goods and where, coincidentally, I needed to find passage to Egypt. We arrived at 11:30 p.m.

Bushed by the terribly long day, I looked for a place to sleep nearby. I started to bed down on the ground between two empty trucks. Just then, I noticed something—rats! There were hundreds of rats scurrying around all over the dock area. I jumped up, grabbed my suitcase, and scrambled up the eight-or-ten-foot sidewall of a truck. I lowered myself down to the truck bed and began to create a makeshift bed using my college warm-up top as a pillow. The bed of the truck was a bad idea; there were more rats. I saw and felt grain seeds on the truck bed, so I knew the rats weren't going anywhere. I climbed out of the truck bed and lowered myself onto the top of the truck cab. I settled there a few minutes to decide if I was safe. Without any food for the rats to eat on top of the cab, they left me alone and I made myself as comfortable as possible under the conditions.

Laying atop the hard metal truck cab above the rat-infested wharf in Beirut, I couldn't help but remember times a decade earlier when my family lived near the alfalfa mill south of the railroad tracks in Holcomb. Six or seven families living there burnt their trash in fifty-five gallon barrels and a makeshift twenty-foot by twenty-foot incinerator. My brother Gary and I, along with neighbor kids, crossed the street and tilted the barrels to watch the rats come out. We had a big, black, mixed-breed Cocker Spaniel named Smokey, and he chased the rats and killed them. He never ate them, but he killed every rat he caught. We'd grab a pipe and beat on the incinerator walls and more rats would come out. As children, we never failed to enjoy watching Smokey chase rats in every which direction while the rats tried to escape and get back under the barrels or the incinerator. In small town Holcomb in the mid-1950s, kids took their fun where they could find it.

I must have been on top of the cab for about forty-five minutes when a security guard, whom I had seen at the customs house about 150 yards away, came strolling over to the truck. With a smile on his face, he motioned for me to come down. Apparently, I would never get to sleep that night. But, the guard surprised me; he took me to an abandoned pick-up truck forty feet from the customs house and invited me to use it for the night. I opened the passenger-side door and carefully checked for rats. Not seeing any, I tossed my suitcase on the floorboard and climbed in. The bench seat in the cab was far more comfortable than many fields and truck-stop floors I had slept on for the last month. This was my "hotel" for the night. My pickup hotel came with an added benefit;

the nearby customs house was open twenty-four hours a day and had a toilet. The security guard let me use the facilities without problems.

As usual, I awoke early and began looking for a ship to Egypt. I received what I thought was misinformation as someone directed me to the Lebanon immigration office. That didn't make a lot of sense to me, so after half-heartedly looking for it for a few minutes, I gave up and returned to the dock area. I had no trouble at all with the police or security guards at the docks and they let me in to make inquiries about which ships were leaving and when and where they were going. I checked with one American ship and eight foreign ships. The American ship was going through the Suez Canal alright, but was not stopping at Egyptian ports. A German ship was going to stop at an Egyptian port, but was not taking passengers. The remaining ships were going to other Mediterranean ports or other destinations around the world. My efforts were beginning to look like Aqaba all over again. Yet, I knew ships made the journey from Beirut to Egypt all the time; I simply needed to find the right ship.

Somewhat discouraged, I took someone's advice and went to downtown Beirut to find a travel agency. I probably should have gone there first, because the first agency knew the Greek passenger ship *Lydia* was going to Egypt that weekend. The *Lydia* wouldn't arrive in Beirut until the next day (Saturday) at 7:00 a.m., and it wouldn't depart until 1:00 p.m. on Sunday afternoon. I had hoped to get out of Beirut much more quickly than that, but the 1:00 p.m. departure on Sunday seemed like the only viable option. There was just one catch—I needed a visa to get into Egypt. The agency refused to sell me a ticket for passage on the boat without the visa. So, I immediately took off for the Egyptian Embassy. I got there quickly enough, only to realize this was Friday, the Islamic holy day. What Sunday is to Christians, Friday is to Muslims. Needless to say, the embassy was closed; I needed to come back the next day.

With nothing to do on a Friday night in Beirut except wait on the Egyptian Embassy to open on Saturday, I went to the movies. I paid just a few cents to see *The Garden of Evil*, a movie I had seen before. The theatre manager let me see a second movie for free, but I don't remember the movie because I slept through the whole thing. Before dark, I returned to the guarded dock and walked the short distance to my pickup hotel. Just as the guard said, my suitcase was safe and sound in the pickup, and that's where I slept my second night in Beirut.

Rarely did I hitchhike within city limits, but after leaving the pickup the next morning, I caught two short rides to the Egyptian Embassy. I arrived just after 7:00 a.m., two full hours before the scheduled opening. That day, the embassy opened at 10:00 a.m., but since I was the first in line, I got through to the correct office immediately. The embassy clerk insisted I come back Monday to get my visa. Under normal circumstances, those directions would be satisfactory. But because the ship left on Sunday afternoon, I vociferously argued with her that coming back on Monday was impossible. An Australian named Bryan overheard the conversation and I soon found out we were both in the same predicament. He also wanted to go to Egypt on Sunday afternoon on the *Lydia*. Together, we pled our case to the clerk and finally got her to agree to see us at 3:00 that afternoon.

With uncommon foresight or sheer luck, on the way out of the embassy, one of us thought to ask the security guard what time the embassy closed on Saturdays. He told us 2:00 p.m. Bryan and I did a smart about-face and hurriedly and brusquely returned to the clerk's office. She was giving us the complete run-around. Caught dead to rights, she finally agreed to see us at 1:30 p.m. After we stepped out and had a quick lunch, we returned to the embassy long before the scheduled meeting time and finally got our visas. I told Bryan if the rest of Egypt was going to treat us as badly as the embassy in Beirut, we ought to skip the whole damn country altogether. Of course if we did that, we'd miss the Nile River, the Sphinx, and the Great Pyramids.

Leaving the Egyptian Embassy, Bryan and I hustled over to the offices of the Hellenic-Mediterranean Lines, the same company that owned the *Appia* on which I sailed from Italy to Greece. After a two-hour delay, we finally bought the cheapest tickets possible—deck-class, for $18.50. I had to cash my next-to-last $20 traveler's check to make the purchase. Bryan returned to his hotel room to pack and I went to a late-afternoon movie.

Getting out of the movie at 6:30 p.m., I walked several

blocks back to the dock area. On the way, I bought a small pocket knife and a couple of pears. I brought another knife from Kansas, a gift from my grandpa solely for the trip, but the other knife was in my suitcase. When I finally got to the gated dock area, I sat down by the gate guard to visit with him and eat the fruit. I made my way over to the pickup and put my passport, boat ticket, and single remaining traveler's check in my suitcase. Still eating the second pear, I bounced up the steps to use the toilet in the customs house, the one I used several times over the previous two or three days. That's when the trouble began.

The friendly customs house guard who directed me to the pickup and provided me with shelter had been replaced by someone new. As I tried to move past the new guard at the top of the steps, he shoved me forcefully and uttered something in Arabic which I took to mean he wasn't going to let me into the customs house. I explained to him carefully I just wanted to use the bathroom, but apparently he didn't understand what I said, knew no English, or didn't care. I tried again to veer around him to get inside the building, but he forcefully shoved me much harder this time and I half stumbled and half fell to the bottom of the stairs. I got madder than hell and raised my arm still holding the half-eaten pear in my right hand. I said to myself, "You sorry son-of-a-bitch, I ought to throw this pear right between your eyes." He thought I was threatening him, so he charged down the stairs, knocked me against a car, and started beating on me. He no sooner started pounding me when another guard joined in and began hitting me on the head, chest, and arms. I dove for the first guy and got in three or four really good blows with my fists. I may have given him a black eye, because a short time later, he was sporting quite a "shiner" that hadn't been there before. Three or four more guards joined the melee and, apparently to save face with their fellow guards, each one had to land a few blows on my head and neck and shoulders. Four of them dragged me into the customs house. All the while, I was screaming all the four-letter expletives I could remember and made up a few new ones along the way.

They sat me down in a chair, but the hitting didn't stop. Every once in a while, a guard walked up behind me and hit me in the back of the head, more a hard, upward slap than a fisted blow seen in a boxing match. Tired of the incessant beating, my temper got the best of me and I once again charged the guard who started the fight in the first place. I knocked him between a filing cabinet and a desk, but his friends quickly came to his rescue. They grabbed me and pushed me into a chair in the corner and three men sat just a few feet away to make sure I didn't continue fighting. I sat there peacefully for about fifteen minutes when a man entered the room wearing civilian clothes. He must have been some high-ranking customs official, because the guards were deferential to him as they explained what had occurred over the last thirty or forty minutes. After their story, the customs official calmly walked over to me, bent over close enough that I could smell his breath and look into his cold, calculating brown eyes. He then slapped me as hard as hell three times before I could react. For the most part, the guards had just been doing their job by trying to keep me in line. But the customs official had attacked me with premeditation and without justification. For decades, the image of his face stayed in my mind, and I fostered an uncompromising hatred for him until the memory faded. Well, so much for divine inspiration and turning the other cheek.

The customs official had three guards take me to the basement where they tossed me into a small room with a dirt floor and a large, heavy wooden door. The room was similar to a medieval dungeon cell I'd seen a hundred times in the movies except it had no window or light of any type. With no windows, it was dark inside and I couldn't see my own hands. I started yelling and screaming and kicking at the door and raising all the commotion possible in hopes of getting out. My antics worked because I was only in there for about ten minutes. The guards dragged me back upstairs and sat me in a chair where I waited more than an hour while they filled out paperwork.

When the paperwork was finished, two guards walked me out of the customs building, down the stairs, and put me in the back of a van. In a short time, they delivered me to a Beirut police station close to the docks and the custom house. Only two policemen were on duty and neither of them attacked me or mistreated me in any way. Without making an ordeal of it, they routinely locked me in a jail cell as if they'd done it a thousand times before. The cell was no different from jail cells found in thousands of cities across America and across the world. Besides mine, there were two more cages. Presumably, it must have been a quiet Saturday night in Beirut, because I was the only prisoner in any of the three cells.

At any rate, the jail cell offered me protection from further attacks. I had time to think and I got worried as hell about two things. First, my suitcase and all my clothes plus my passport, boat ticket, and a traveler's check were in the old pickup back at the docks. Without a friendly guard on the customs house steps, I just knew someone would steal the suitcase and all its contents. If the guard that started the whole confrontation knew my suitcase was in the pickup, he'd take it just for spite if nothing else. Secondly, I had no idea how long I'd be in jail—a day, a week, a month, or more? Even though it seemed like ages ago, I had bought passage on the *Lidia* that afternoon and the ship was going to sail to Egypt on Sunday at 1:00 p.m., with or without me. I had gotten myself into a tough situation, but I rationalized it wasn't my fault; the fault lay with the new guard. Regardless of whose fault it was, the ship was scheduled to leave in fourteen or fifteen hours.

I remained in the jail cell for more than an hour when a man from the American Embassy arrived. He listened to what I had to say, concluded it was simply a great misunderstanding, then chided me harshly for threatening a Lebanese customs officer. He also advised me to be much more cautious with my attitude and my actions around police and security officials. The American signed some papers and the police released me, but they confiscated my newly purchased pocket knife and fined me fifteen cents. That must have been the standard fine for threatening an assault on a customs official with a pear. The strangest thing about the entire ordeal was the whole time I was held at both the customs house and the police station, no one ever asked me for my passport. Apparently, the officials were satisfied with the identification shown on my Kansas driver's license.

When I walked out of the police station, I was so mentally, emotionally, and physically exhausted I could have dropped to the concrete sidewalk and slept soundly until morning. But I had to retrieve my suitcase and its valuable contents—if they were still there. Tired and almost in a daze, I made the trek back to the docks and the gate guard let me in long enough to walk to the pickup. By the grace of God, the suitcase was still there. I retrieved it and left the dock to where a truck driver a few blocks away let me sleep in the back of his parked truck.

It was well after sun-up when I left the truck and dashed off to the docks to catch the ship. On the way, I stopped at a hotel and talked the clerk into letting me take a shower. I gave him thirty cents for the privilege and watched him stick the money in his pocket as I started for the room. Since it had been four or five days since I had last showered (I was too tired to remember exactly), I thought my fellow passengers on board ship would appreciate me more if I didn't smell like a garbage dump.

The hot water felt good enough that I could have stayed an hour, but I had a ship to catch. Changing into fresh clothes, I continued my route to the docks. With a fresh shower and the excitement of leaving Lebanon, I was feeling good—good enough to stop and watch a game of three-card Monte. I let myself get suckered in and lost $1.25 before I realized I had been conned. In the overall scheme of things, it was a cheap lesson, but in the financial predicament I was in at the time, $1.25 was a lot of money.

It was a good thing I didn't dally longer at the hotel or the sidewalk card game, because once I got to the ship, they told me before I boarded, I had to first check out of Lebanon. It dawned on me someone tried to give me that information three days earlier, but at that time, I had given up looking for the immigration office. This time, with more precise directions and with my suitcase in hand, I trudged the few blocks to the immigration office and "officially" exited Lebanon.

The *Lydia*, officially the *MS Lydia I*, was built in 1931 and for nearly twenty-five years operated as a cruise ship for the Adelaide Steamship Company between ports in Australia. In 1955, she was sold to the Hellenic-Mediterranean Lines, transferred to the Mediterranean Sea, and regularly stopped in a dozen ports in southern Europe and North Africa. The route from Beirut to Port Said, Egypt was only one leg of a much longer cruise. The ship's top speed was thirteen knots or about sixteen miles an hour.

When I finally boarded the *Lydia*, I must have been the last passenger to do so, because the ship pulled away from the dock less than thirty minutes after I arrived. My ticket was for "deck-class", therefore, I looked around on the deck for a good place to sit or lie down. The deck-class passengers had been herded onto the foredeck, and since I was late getting on board, all the good spots had been taken. In fact, it seemed someone was camped out on every square inch of available space. I thought there were four or five hundred people on deck. Later, I was told only 255 paid for deck class, but I seriously doubted that much smaller number. Luckily, I spotted Bryan on deck and by maneuvering some backpacks and other luggage, I was able to wedge in next to him for the ride to Egypt. Over the course of the next two hours, I told him of my fiasco at the customs house and police station.

Deck-class on a Greek ship is exactly that; passengers are on deck with no privileges to go anywhere below deck. Only one bathroom for men and another for women served the hundreds of deck-class passengers. No meals were served to these passengers, but a small snack bar—more like a concession stand at a high school football game—provided expensive food items to keep anyone from starving. Most passengers had food and bottled drinks stored in their backpacks. Not me, I wasn't smart enough to think that far ahead.

Although I wasn't smart enough to think about buying food in preparation for the voyage, I was perceptive enough to notice an absence of life jackets. Life jackets were clearly visible on both ferries across the English Channel and on the *Appia* when I crossed the Adriatic Sea from Italy to Greece. I certainly didn't see any life jackets on the *Lydia*, and although there were probably some around somewhere, I had serious doubts whether there were enough for everyone on board, particularly those of us on deck-class. Both the *Tide* and the *Appia* also conducted "mandatory" life-boat drills—the *Lydia* did not. I could see the newspaper headlines now, "Greek Ship Overturns in Eastern Mediterranean Storm, 540 Feared Lost at Sea." Later, I learned the maximum capacity for deck-class passengers on the *Lydia* was 180. On the day of my voyage to Egypt, the *Lydia* transported far more than 180 people on the deck. No wonder they didn't conduct a life-boat drill.

There was far less to do and it was far more boring as a deck-class passenger than it had been on the *Tide*. At least on the *Tide*, I went to my room, took a shower, ate three good meals a day, and played cribbage or bridge in the evening. The only activities possible on this voyage were sleeping and thinking, and when I thought, I reflected on the circumstances I had gone through during the previous night in Beirut.

I always possessed a fiery temper and was often quick to anger; a characteristic inherited from the paternal side of the family for at least two generations. But I never got into fights, certainly none of consequence. Being small for my age, if I had I fought my peers, they would have kicked the hell out of me. I excelled at high school debate and was, without question, argumentative to a fault, but my combative nature never led to fisticuffs—until the Beirut incident. The ordeal revealed a part of me I didn't know myself.

None of the many hits the guards inflicted on me were all that painful and I didn't turn black and blue. And none of the injuries drew blood except when the civilian slapped me in the face and cut the left corner of my mouth. But I was sore as I sat there with Bryan floating slowly toward Egypt. All in all, it might have turned out much worse. Had I been an older adult, or had the incident occurred ten or twenty or thirty years later, I'm sure they'd have shot me first and asked questions later—or at least incarcerated me for an extended period of time. Either of those scenarios would have been life-ending or life-changing experiences. I do know that after the Beirut episode, I was mentally and psychologically more hardened, more calloused, and less naïve than before. Unlike my days in Bethlehem, after Beirut, I didn't feel as close to God.

Even though we deck-class passengers were completely exposed to the elements for the entire eighteen-hour trip, it didn't rain on us and we didn't get into a storm. A little after 7:00 a.m. on Monday, July 26 th, the *Lydia* docked at Port Said, Egypt.

Crossing Egypt (Twice)

After Bryan and I settled on the deck of the *Lydia*, we began checking out the other passengers. I was the first to spot Jenny. She stood about five foot four and weighed a little more than 100 pounds. She wore her hair tied up in the back in a pony-tail style, except the hair didn't fall much below her neck. On the boat, she wore her hair tucked under a faded but typical olive-drab Australian bush hat—one side-brim tied up and the other hanging down. On the open sea, she needed the hat to protect her from the sun and to keep her cool. Her hair was red, about two shades darker than my own. Typical with many red-haired people, Jenny had beautiful green eyes, noticeable halfway across the deck. She also had freckles; a few on her cheeks and more on her lower neck and breasts—a least as far down as was possible to see. And she was attractive—not beautiful in the true sense of the word, but nice looking. When I first saw her on the boat, I was more attracted to her than I had been to Grace, the blond nurse I spent three days with in Greece.

Bryan and I made a point to befriend this twenty-year-old Australian girl. Except when one of us was sleeping, the three of us visited and swapped stories during the entire cruise. When she was awake, our visits were often interrupted by her frequent trips to the bathroom. A few days earlier, she had come down with dysentery, probably from drinking dirty water. When leaving the ship, she joined us during the nearly three hours it took to clear Egyptian customs and immigration. (Coincidentally, when Bryan and I set foot on Egyptian soil, Africa became the fourth continent for both of us. He had not been to North or South America or Antarctica. I had not been to South America, Australia, or Antarctica.) Jenny suggested we go to a travel agency to find the best way to get to Cairo. The travel agency informed us the least expensive way to get from Port Said to Cairo was by train. I cashed my last $20 traveler's check and bought a train ticket to Cairo for $1.16.

For several miles, the train tracks ran parallel to the Suez Canal—the very canal I tried desperately to get to those three frustrating days in Aqaba. The Suez Canal, opened almost a hundred years before (1869), is a sea-level canal wholly within Egypt that connects the Mediterranean Sea and the Red Sea. Suez allows ships travelling between Europe and Asia to avoid the much longer distance around the Cape of Good Hope at the south end of Africa. For ships small enough to navigate through it, the Panama Canal in the Western Hemisphere serves the same purpose, except ships are avoiding the long trip and treacherous waters of Cape Horn around the south end of South America. The 120-mile long Suez Canal is much more efficient than the Panama Canal because the former is a free-flowing channel without locks and several passing lanes along the route.

During the first few miles of the train ride, we saw more than a dozen ships on the canal. A strange and amusing sight unfolded. The roadbed for the railway was lower than the raised, sandy-banked sides of the canal, so often times, the canal water was invisible from our vantage point. For all intents and purposes, it appeared the giant ships were moving on top of the desert sand. It was impossible to anticipate then, but I would experience the same feeling of disbelief nearly three years later when I was taking jungle training in Panama on my way to Vietnam. During daytime maneuvers, I peeked through dense Panamanian jungle and saw an enormous cargo ship no more than one hundred feet away. The freighter scared the hell out of me and if the ship had tooted its fog horn before I saw it, I might have died of fright!

The train to Cairo operated like a New York subway by stopping at every village and train stop along the way. So it was 5:00 p.m. when we finally arrived in Cairo, by far the largest city in Africa. Jenny found an affordable hotel nearby, but Bryan wanted to check out the local YMCA, thinking that might be the least expensive place for us to stay. Jenny said during her travels, she had stayed at the YWCA and several youth hostels, but this late in the evening, all the beds would be taken. We said goodbye to her and Bryan and I walked a few blocks to the YMCA. When we got there, we found out Jenny was right; all the beds had been booked for the night. We trudged our way back to the hotel Jenny had selected where he and I shared a hotel room for $1.00 apiece.

I hadn't had anything substantial to eat for a day or two, so Bryan and I slipped out of the hotel and found a nearby restaurant. The restaurant was packed with people; always a good sign when you're traveling. We waited for about five minutes for a table and then had an Egyptian dish made of rice, corn, and beans. We topped it off with rice pudding, all for less than twenty-five cents. Full and contented, we returned to the hotel, stopping on the way to buy Cokes and wafers for an evening snack.

I had just finished washing some clothes in the bathtub when someone knocked on the door. If it wasn't the hotel maid, it had to be Jenny. She was the only person in Cairo who knew we were there. Indeed, it was Jenny and she wanted to talk to us.

Jenny was from Perth, Australia. She had flown to England and was hitchhiking back home. From our conversations on the ship, Bryan and I knew that after visiting Egypt, she wanted to return to Beirut by ship, and then hitchhike home by way of Syria, Iraq, Iran, India, Pakistan, and Indonesia. Even though she had made it from London to Cairo on her own, she now had second thoughts about traveling alone through several Islamic countries. She came to ask if either Bryan or I or both would join her. Perhaps she had thought of asking us before, but she didn't mention it anytime on the cruise from Beirut.

As a fellow Australian, Bryan sympathized with her but told her quickly he simply couldn't go. He was going to spend a few days in Cairo, then head south on the Nile to Khartoum. Once he returned to Cairo, he planned on crossing North Africa using the same route I was going to use. On the other hand, my travel plans were more flexible and I had no specific time to be at any specific place. The truth was, however, I was almost out of money. I didn't have enough for passage to return from Egypt to Beirut. Jenny asked me to call my folks and have them wire two or three hundred dollars through Western Union or to the Cairo American Express office. Surely, the money would arrive in a day or two and then we could be off together. That decision may have been the most difficult one for me on my entire trip and her offer was enticing. But I knew getting home to Kansas from Cairo was much shorter going west than going by way of India and Australia. Not only that, but if I joined her, I would miss the fall semester at college. Ever since I left the Holy Land, I thought about returning home to start school in the fall. I told Jenny I doubted I'd join her, but I would think about it and let her know the following day.

I tossed and turned that night thinking about traveling to Australia with Jenny. I got up before Bryan and wrote two long letters home while I waited for him. Once he was up and dressed, we knocked on Jenny's door, but she was too sick to join us. We grabbed a bite to eat at a nearby café, mailed the letters, and looked for a travel agency. Bryan wanted to check on fares and schedules for trips up the Nile. Once he gathered the information, we left the travel agency and went to the Egyptian Museum of Antiquities. The museum houses the world's largest collection of Egyptian relics, including many treasures of

King Tutankhamen. As you might imagine, we saw mummies, sarcophagi (stone coffins), ancient golden jewelry, and other Egyptian artifacts dated hundreds, perhaps thousands of years before Christ.

In the afternoon, we paid ten cents for a taxi ride to take us to the Great Pyramids and the Sphinx, located twelve miles west of Cairo. The Great Pyramid of Giza is the oldest and largest of the three pyramids and is also the oldest of the Seven Wonders of the Ancient World. For 3,800 years, the Great Pyramid was also the tallest structure in the world. Like millions of tourists before me, I wondered how they went about moving and placing more than two million stone blocks weighing from twenty-five to eighty tons each. As I stood there in awe, I judged this structure as the second-most impressive sight I'd seen on my trip falling one step behind the grandeur of the Swiss Alps.

Climbing on the Great Pyramid was forbidden, so that's exactly what we did. We didn't climb far. Each stone is about four-and-a-half-feet high and I found it difficult to pull myself up after more than two or three stones. Climbing down was just as difficult. We soon gave up our climbing efforts and decided to take an easier route—inside the pyramid itself.

The Great Pyramid is the only one in the area with a passageway inside. Climbing the ascending passage to the King's Chamber high in the pyramid proved long and arduous. The passageway is small enough a grown person cannot stand up while ascending or descending the stairs.

As small as I am, I still found the climbing difficult and the poor lighting made me claustrophobic. I couldn't wait to get out of the passageway and onto a level floor. Bryan and I finally reached the King's Chamber; a small room about fifteen by thirty feet with a twenty-foot ceiling. Dark polished granite lined the walls and ceiling and the only item in the room was a single rectangular granite sarcophagus with one broken corner. No skeletal remains or contents of any kind were in the coffin itself, nor was there a lid on the coffin or anywhere in the room. The sides of the sarcophagus were more than four feet high. Bryan and I were convinced it had not been hauled up the stairs we just climbed. The coffin must have been placed in the chamber before completion of the pyramid. After the narrow, constricted stairway, the chamber felt downright spacious. I was happy I took the time and effort to go inside the pyramid, but hurried out to the comfort of the desert outside. We descended the same way we went in.

Once outside, Bryan wanted to walk around all four sides of the pyramid. I told him one side of a pyramid looks just like the other three. He answered my flippant remark with a smirk and began his quest. I ambled off in the other direction and about five minutes later, a young boy about ten or eleven years old motioned for me to follow him. He led me to a small cave or opening in a structure long-buried by desert sand. We slithered through a small gap and after waiting for our eyes to adjust to the darkness, we crawled on our hands and knees about fifteen feet to reach a topless, wooden coffin.

Inside was a complete skeleton; how old, I had no clue. Before I peeked, I prepared myself mentally for that occurrence, so it didn't scare me as much as it might have. My fear focused on the roof caving in, so in less than two minutes, we slinked back outside to stand in the sunshine. The boy held out his hand and I gave him ten cents for the experience.

I caught up with Bryan and we walked the short distance to look closely at the Great Sphinx. Cut out of solid stone and facing due east, the Sphinx is an impressive sight in its own right, with the body of a lion and the head of a human. Although unproven, artillery rounds may have removed the nose of the Sphinx and marred its beauty. Historians remain unsure who to blame for this destruction; some say Napoleon while others name the Ottoman Turks.

I crossed the Nile River in the taxi on the way to the pyramids and again on the return trip to the hotel. At over 4,100 miles and running through ten countries, the Nile is the longest river in the world. Before the construction of the High Aswan Dam in the 1950s, the Nile flooded each year and the untamed waters were a sight to behold as far north as Cairo and beyond. Although it's the longest river, the Nile pales in significance after a person sees the Amazon.

I saw the Nile, the Pyramids, and the Sphinx—what else was there to do in Egypt? One more thing—a few hundred yards from the Sphinx and for only a quarter, I rode a camel. The camel ride proved more uncomfortable than riding a Shetland pony at a trot and smelled a hell of a lot worse. Despite my negative comments about the ride, it's the one situation on my trip that I wish I captured in a photo.

During the taxi ride back to the hotel, I told Bryan about the wooden coffin and skeleton the young boy had shown me. Bryan suggested the boy's father placed the coffin and skeleton in the cave the previous week so his kids could lure unsuspecting tourists like me. If so, the scheme worked and Bryan and I both had a good laugh about it.

We returned to the hotel after 4:00 p.m. I took a quick shower and went down the hallway to give Jenny my answer about the trip to Australia. I told her I wouldn't be going with her. She understood and told me that she was now considering bypassing Syria, Iraq, and Iran and flying to India and hitchhiking to Australia from there. Jenny was still in the grips of dysentery and the only traveling she planned on doing was from the bed to the bathroom. I wished her luck with her health and her travels and returned to my room to grab my suitcase and say goodbye to Bryan. I truly enjoyed traveling and spending time with the two of them the last few days.

I rode a city bus to the north edge of Cairo and contemplated my situation. I had less than twenty dollars in my pocket and 9,000 miles separated me from my home in Kansas. I knew there were few hotel rooms and few good meals in my future as I traversed across the north coast of Africa. I needed to get from Cairo to

Alexandria and from there westward to Libya. I had not hitchhiked since I arrived in Beirut some six days earlier. Before nightfall, I caught a truck ride halfway to Alexandria. A second truck took me into the city and the driver dropped me off at 5:00 a.m.

I grabbed a small breakfast in Alexandria and then a van driver gave me a lift to the west edge of town. In northern Egypt, the road west to Libya hugs the Mediterranean Sea. Since no deep-water ports of any significance are found west of Alexandria, few villages and towns exist along the road. A single car ride took me just north of the Qattara Depression and another forty miles to El Alamein, the site of two major battles between the British Commonwealth forces and the German-Italian forces in World War II. In the first battle, in August 1942, German General Erwin Rommel tried to stop the Allied advance into Africa. Two months later, with British General Bernard Montgomery in charge, an Allied victory ended the German threat to Egypt, the Suez Canal, and access to the Middle Eastern oil fields. Significantly, the Second Battle of Alamein was the first major offensive against the Germans in which the Western Allies achieved a decisive victory.

Far removed from the carnage of a quarter century earlier, I found myself stuck on the west side of El Alamein for more than five hours. Late in the afternoon, I arrived at the coastal town of Marsa Matruh, where I sat by the side of the road until dark. A friendly Egyptian farmer stopped and gave me a whole watermelon and some flat bread. With only two rides all day outside city limits, this was the worst hitchhiking day of my trip. Having no sleep the night before, I didn't care much. I sauntered a few yards away from the road and slept the night in the Sahara Desert. It wouldn't be my last night sleeping in the Sahara.

When I awoke the next morning, I did something highly unusual for me: I walked a mile or so down the road before I sat on my suitcase and waited for a ride. No cars or trucks stopped, but a crowded bus did and the driver let me ride for free. There was barely room for me and my suitcase. Several seats in the back had boards across the aisle to allow another person or two to sit instead of standing during the long trip. The ride was terribly uncomfortable and hot for the human passengers, but more uncomfortable for the dozen chickens trapped inside reed baskets and the lambs on the floor between their owner's feet. I was happy to get a free bus ride, but happier when he delivered me directly to the Libyan border.

I cleared Egyptian immigration without problems, but Libya wouldn't let me cross their border without a visa. I had to purchase a visa at a Libyan Embassy or Consulate office, and the closest one was over 300 miles east, in Alexandria. I had no choice but to retrace my steps and buy a Libyan visa.

At the Egyptian immigration office on the Libyan border, I had checked out of Egypt but not checked into Libya. In essence, I was in no man's land. I caught an eastbound ride in a car—the fastest on the trip. The driver hurled us down the highway and took me the entire 300 miles back to Alexandria. Despite the quick five-hour ride, I was terribly tired. At a gas station I snacked and guzzled a Coke then asked the attendant if he had a place I could sleep. He offered a flattened cardboard box in a corner of a back room and that's where I spent the night.

Before the night attendant got off duty, he gave me directions to the Libyan Consulate office—about a half-hour walk from the gas station. Since it was too early for them to be open, I shunned a taxi and walked the entire distance with suitcase in hand. The moment I saw the "Closed" sign, it dawned on me. This was Friday, and like every Islamic embassy or consulate office, they were closed. After surviving the one-day delay in Lebanon the previous Friday, I cursed myself for failing to realize the day of the week. I was especially angry at myself for carrying my suitcase unnecessarily for thirty minutes.

I was also frustrated and disappointed with myself for failing to check the requirements for a Libyan visa while in Cairo. At this stage in the game, I'd simply have to wait until the next day. That gave me a full day and night to kill in Alexandria. With little money, my options were limited. I stopped at a candy store and struck up a conversation with a young lady with great English skills. I told her I was killing time while waiting for the Libyan Consulate office to open the next day. She let me stow my suitcase behind the counter. For fifteen cents, I went to an early afternoon movie, *Cheyenne Autumn*, starring Richard

Widmark. After the movie, I returned to the candy store to check on my suitcase. All was okay, so I returned to the same theatre for the late afternoon movie, *The Ten Gladiators*, and the ticket vendor let me in for free. After the second movie, I again checked on my suitcase. At a sidewalk café I enjoyed a couple of Cokes while reading an English newspaper, the first newspaper I had read since Rome.

In the evening I saw *My Fair Lady* with Rex Harrison and Audrey Hepburn. I fell in love with Audrey Hepburn —or was it Eliza Doolittle? In either case, the movie became my favorite musical and remained my favorite for four decades—until I heard the music from *Les Miserables*. In Alexandria, *My Fair Lady* played in English with Arabic subtitles. A movie about speaking poor English doesn't translate well into another language and I was the only person laughing in the whole theatre. I'm sure my laughing annoyed the other patrons, but they were annoyed with me anyway. I failed to stand up when the theatre played the Egyptian national anthem before the movie began. I received a lot of dirty looks when I remained seated.

All "movied" out, I returned to the candy store for the fourth time. The young lady had gone home, but my suitcase was still there as were two young men my age. A quick conversation with an English-speaking Sudanese boy led him to invite me to his house for the night. As is the case with ninety percent of the homes in this part of the world, family members often sleep outside on the top of the building's flat roof. With three or four foot sidewalls all around, the roof-top "veranda" offers privacy and much-needed extra space for the residents. That's where the three of us ended up soon after we arrived. I was offered a prayer rug or *sajada* to sleep on. I made myself comfortable and within ten minutes, the friend of the Sudanese boy tried to accost me. I must have been getting inured to homosexual advances because I shouted at him to leave me alone so I could sleep. He did and I did.

When the Libyan Embassy opened at 10:00 on Saturday morning, I had been waiting for more than thirty minutes. Shortly, I stepped into the office that issued the visas. They told me in no uncertain terms they issued no visas on Saturday and I needed to come back on Monday. To say I was highly upset or distraught understated the situation. I was pissed! I needed a Libyan visa and would get it even if I had to call in the cavalry.

In most major cities, embassy or consulate buildings for various countries are located in the same general section of the city. That was true in Alexandria as the American Consulate office was only six blocks away. Without problems, I entered the office and a polite young woman, Vicki Dunlap, greeted me and asked how she might help. Still visibly upset, I asked her if the State Department could fly me to Europe and I would pay them back later. Her soothing nature calmed me down a bit and I revealed the real crux of my problem. I was nearly destitute and didn't have the money to wait around in Alexandria (or anyplace else for that matter) while the Libyans stalled on issuing me a visa. From her filing cabinet, she grabbed a form letter with an American Consulate letterhead and typed a few sentences indicating I was a college student and needed to get through Libya. She then picked up the phone and talked to someone for less than a minute. Vicki then advised me to return to the Libyan Consulate office, which I did as quickly as possible. Whether it was the letter or the phone call or because I was a student, thirty minutes later, I had my visa to enter Libya. The visa fee was two dollars, but the Libyans issued it to me without cost. I was so grateful about the turn of events, I took the time to return to the American Consulate office and personally thank Vicki for her competence and efficiency.

For the rest of the day and for many days afterward, I thought about the different treatment I had received at the Egyptian Embassy in Beirut and the Libyan Consulate office in Alexandria compared to the American Consulate office in Alexandria. In the two Arabic offices, I was met with indifference with absolutely no desire on their part to solve my problems. Incompetence and procrastination seemed the order of the day. If it was simply an attitude toward Americans or toward me, I don't know. But after the excellent, professional treatment I received at the American Consulate office, I saw the contrast between the mindsets of different countries and how they address similar problems differently. The contrast was stark and I vowed to be much more wary when I had future dealings with other countries' consulates. In retrospect, the delay was my own fault because I could have obtained the visa in Cairo before I left.

Two short bus rides and two short car rides put me back on the outskirts of Marsa Matruh at the exact spot I had stood looking for a ride three days earlier. Since it was late in the afternoon and I was too tired to hitchhike anymore that day, I walked back into town to grab a bite to eat. I found out I could get to the Egyptian border town of Saloom cheaply by taking the train. That sounded like a wonderful idea, but the train didn't leave until early the next morning. So, dragging my suitcase along, I did what I always did to spend an evening in Egyptian towns: I went to a movie. The theatre was just like a drive-in movie—except there were no cars. A hundred folding chairs had been set up in an open-air enclosure. Apparently, rain fell so infrequently in that part of the desert that a roof was unnecessary. The locals and I watched Glenn Ford in *The Fastest Gun Alive* and when the movie got out, I went to the train depot where I slept the night.

I awoke only ten minutes before the train left and then hurriedly bought my ticket; a second-class ticket for fifty cents. Since less than 150 miles remained between me and the Libyan border, I figured to make it in three or four hours, possibly less. I figured wrong. The train stopped to deliver water seemingly every ten or fifteen minutes. On several of the stops, there were no villages or towns, just people queued up to fill water containers. Even when the train reached top speed, I felt I could have gotten out and run alongside without losing ground. To make matters worse, the railway was several miles distant from the highway in which I had hitchhiked in both directions a few days before. Consequently, I didn't feel confident about jumping off the train and hiking through the Sahara looking for the highway next to the Mediterranean Sea. Simply put, I was stuck on the train for what turned out to be fifteen minutes less than ten hours—a whopping fifteen miles an hour. So much for sidewalk-café travel tips in Marsa Matruh, Egypt.

During the train ride, a young boy approached me with a handful of ancient coins. Certainly, I was no numismatic expert, but the coins sure appeared authentic to me. I looked them over carefully, all twelve of them and decided I'd buy them from him. Well, "buy" was the wrong word, because I didn't have the extra money. I opened my suitcase and showed him my bright yellow college warm-up top. His eyes brightened immediately and I knew we had a trade. I figured the last thing I needed in the Sahara Desert was a fleece warm-up top. He was happy and I was happy and neither one of us knew who got the better end or worse end of the deal. (To this day, I still have the coins and have dated one definitively as a late eighth century Greek coin.)

The train stopped in Saloom, Egypt, still some four or five miles short of the Libyan frontier. I hopped a bus and rode the ten minutes from the train station to the Egyptian-Libyan border. This time, I had no trouble with customs or immigration from either country.

I had spent almost seven full days in Egypt, more than twice as long as I had intended and far longer than other places on my trip except the Holy Land. Once I said goodbye to the three nurses in Athens, I was anxious and happy to leave Greece. Once I had the run-in with the customs officials in Beirut, I was more than anxious and happy to leave Lebanon. And now that I had spent way too much time in embassies and the boring Egyptian desert, I was thrilled to leave Egypt. Mentally and physically fatigued, I looked forward to spending a few quiet and restful days in Benghazi with the parents of a high school classmate.

Libya and a Strange Night in Benghazi

I rode a bus westward from the Libyan border for about 140 miles. Then I caught a short ride with a truck driver who took me toward Tobruk. When he stopped, the driver gave me a blanket and I slept the night in a field about six miles east of Tobruk.

In my college history classes and in movies, I heard of Tobruk and the deadly battles that took place there. After sleeping in the field east of town, I quickly got a ride and had the driver drop me off downtown instead of taking me through town and onto Benghazi. On my way into town, I noticed a number of escarpments and cliffs south of the city. When World War II began, Libya was an Italian colony and those impenetrable cliffs around Tobruk prevented the Allies from capturing the city easily and quickly by land. But capture it they did. Even though the Italians had heavily fortified Tobruk before their invasion of Egypt in November 1940, the British, Australian, and Indian forces captured the city in January 1941. Like a bloody and deathly tennis match, the Germans, under an attack led by Rommel in May 1942, re-captured the city (the Battle of Gazala) and held it until November 1942. The last volley occurred when the Allies re-captured Tobruk during the Second Battle of El Alamein and it remained in Allied hands thereafter.

While I was having a breakfast of crackers and a Coke, I thought I'd take a few extra hours to visit Rommel's Gazala battlefield south of town. While I sat in the café, I made inquiries about the site and two different people advised me to avoid going out there. They seemed to think there were hundreds or thousands of unexploded land mines all over the battlefield. Naturally, with both the Axis and Allied powers having held Tobruk over a five-or six-year period, both sides planted land mines throughout the war. I didn't need to make further inquiries; I bypassed visiting a battle site where I might accidentally step on a German or British land mine.

The Sahara Desert, the world's largest, is almost 3,200 miles across. I didn't travel the entire distance, but certainly travelled most of it. Libya makes up a good portion of the Sahara, much of which is remote and perishingly hot. In fact, Libya holds the world record (1922) for hottest air temperature with a reading of 136°. That record, however, is disputed by the modern-day meteorological community. Happily, it wasn't that hot in the first week of August 1965 when I traveled the principal road that parallels Libya's Mediterranean Sea coastline. Nonetheless, the temperature was hot enough I wanted to avoid getting caught in the daytime in an isolated spot in the middle of nowhere. From Egypt to Tunisia I had to cross more than 1,100 miles of Libya, and I figured it would take me several days, particularly if I stopped in Benghazi for three or four days at the home of my friend's parents.

After I left Tobruk, I had traveled only 145 miles of the 1,100 miles across Libya. My first car ride of the day took me over 100 miles where I was let out in a small town. As I stopped at a café for a bite to eat, an obviously mentally disturbed man approached me and gave me the Libyan equivalent of thirty-five cents for no apparent reason. Then, I thought, he might have wanted my blanket the truck driver had given me a few nights before. I gave him the blanket and he went happily on his way. Later, the waitress told me the man had gone crazy because he accidentally killed his best friend many years earlier. I'm glad I gave him the blanket.

I quickly got a car ride with a Libyan who taught high school English. The conversation between us turned out to be the most fascinating and memorable one I had on my entire trip. Our talk also strongly influenced me. After we exchanged basic information and pleasantries, he told me he might be getting married the next Saturday. Even though he was an English teacher, I wondered if I had lost something in translation. I asked him directly what he meant by "might" be getting married. With only six days before the wedding, how could he fail to know if he was getting married or not? He then explained he was already married—to two wives—and this marriage on Saturday was to be to his third wife. Six days ahead of time, the details hadn't yet been worked out between their families. The upcoming marriage was an arranged one and he and the young girl had only met on three previous occasions. He informed me that under Islamic law, and confirmed in several passages in the Koran, a Muslim may take up to four wives as long as he has the financial means to do so. The teacher further explained to me he was sufficiently well-off to afford three wives and hoped someday to have the full complement of four. (Being single and only eighteen years old at the time, I couldn't have known that I, too, would have three or four wives—just not at the same time.)

Captivated by the two-hour conversation we had, I was particularly absorbed in the aspect of polygamy. The conversation influenced me so much that while working on my bachelor's degree in 1973, I focused on Mormonism and the role polygamy played in the life of Joseph Smith, the founder of Mormonism. Later, Joseph Smith, Mormonism, and polygamy became a part of my academic emphasis in the 1980s while doing post-graduate work. To think while most of life's interests are gathered from friends, family members, or high school teachers, my concentration in that field began with a car ride with a stranger west of Tobruk, Libya.

During my trip, I had hundreds of rides and conversations, but only a handful were interesting or fascinating. I was truly sorry when this ride came to an end in the teacher's hometown of Bayda. He took extra time to take me to the west edge of town so I wouldn't be stuck in city traffic. From that side of town it was much easier to catch a ride to Benghazi. The teacher's kindness continued to amaze me when he handed me the equivalent of $1.50—a real blessing as broke as I was. His gift not only represented enough money for me to eat for a day or two, but also enough to get a night in a hotel too. I was thrilled! I thanked him effusively and wished him well on his "maybe" wedding.

Only a few small towns dot the roadway between Bayda and Benghazi, and thankfully, my next ride bypassed all of them. I arrived in Benghazi at 4:00 p.m. and rushed directly to the American Consulate office. I knew my friend's parents lived in Benghazi, but another 150,000 people lived there as well. I hoped the Consulate office would give me the address for Mr. Greg Parker and his wife. They did. An hour later, I knocked on their apartment door, but my heart sank; no one was at home. What if they were on vacation in the US or somewhere else? Just as I was about to leave, a neighbor across the hall stuck her head outside her apartment door and told me the Parker's weren't home. (I knew that already.) She added the husband was working, but the wife would be home later. She advised me to come back in the evening. There wasn't much else I could do, so I walked around the streets of Benghazi until nearly 7:30 p.m. before I returned to the apartment. This time, the wife was home.

Mrs. Parker—her given name was Genevieve but she said everyone just called her Gina— invited me inside. She also invited me to call her Gina instead of Mrs. Parker and even though it made me uncomfortable, I went along with her request.

Mrs. Parker, I mean Gina, was of medium height and build with short, dishwater-blond hair. Although I have always been a poor judge of a person's age, I guessed she might have been in her early or mid-forties. Perhaps she was older than that because her glasses didn't hide the wrinkles around and below her eyes and the laugh lines at both corners of her mouth. She was not overweight or voluptuous by any means, but more full-figured than either Grace or Jenny. She wore no makeup, but she might have removed it before I arrived. She was barefooted and was wearing a comfortable pair of shorts and tank top. Unlike the last woman I saw wearing a tank top—the French girl I saw when I arrived in Greece—Gina was wearing a bra. I knew this because the straps on her bra and the straps on her tank top didn't match up. Just like my parents, Gina smoked heavily. During our entire evening conversation, even during the meal, she seldom let a cigarette escape her lips. She also drank gin and tonic liberally and offered to fix me one, but I declined.

Gina welcomed me with warmth and friendliness and appeared to be genuinely glad to see me. She confirmed immediately the neighbor was right; Greg was working in the oil fields in the Sahara far south of Benghazi. He worked three weeks in the desert, then one week back in town. She added he was scheduled to be in the desert for several more days. They had been in Libya for almost a year now, and even though both she and Greg had become accustomed to the unusual work schedule, it didn't make it any less boring. She apparently tried to fight the boredom by drinking heavily and probably drank six or eight gin and tonics during the course of the evening.

Gina and I met once before—at her daughter Sarah's sixteenth birthday party two or three years earlier. Since I was only one of thirty teenagers at the party, I sincerely doubted she remembered me. As she cooked supper, we had a pleasant conversation primarily focused on my travels and the things I had seen. She said, unfortunately, she and Greg hadn't been anyplace but Libya from the time they arrived. I tried to get more information from her about Sarah, but the only thing I found out was Sarah and her boyfriend had moved from Kansas to California. Back in high school, Sarah told me several times that she and her mother were never close. Remembering those school conversations, I didn't press the point so we talked about other things. I thoroughly enjoyed the pork chops, baked potato, and corn Gina prepared. That supper was the first home-cooked meal I had since Bethlehem and the first (and only) home-cooked American meal on my trip.

It was after 10:00 p.m. when we finished eating. Gina said she was tired and sleepy and I could tell she was a little woozy from the alcohol. She added that she didn't want to be a rude hostess, but asked me if it was okay if she went to bed early. I said of course and added that I wasn't sleepy yet and thought I might go out for a few minutes and get a Coke. She answered okay, handed me her apartment key, and said to let myself in whenever I returned. I found a nearby sidewalk café and sat there and enjoyed the quiet, still Libyan evening while drinking a couple of Cokes. As I sat there, I reflected that between the conversation with the English teacher and the excellent home-cooked meal, the day had been a most satisfying one. My thoughts, however, kept coming back to the English teacher and his multiple wives. I vowed to investigate further into this unusual social practice whenever I had the opportunity.

When I returned and let myself in, the one-bedroom apartment was dark except for a small kitchen light. At the end of the sofa, my bed for the night, I fumbled through my suitcase and found my toothbrush and headed for the bathroom. The bathroom and the bedroom were right beside each other and the bedroom door was wide-open. With an outside street light strongly illuminating the bedroom, I saw Gina sleeping soundly on her back completely nude. I ducked into the bathroom, brushed my teeth, and went to the toilet. The sound of the water running in the sink and toilet didn't awaken her, because when I came out of the bathroom, she was in exactly the same position. She was either in a deep sleep, passed out, or both. I lingered at the bedroom doorway for five or ten seconds then returned to the sofa to bed down for the night. I must have developed early stages of prostrate problems that night, because I visited the bathroom fifteen or twenty times before morning. (No, wait...that was just a joke.) The sofa was comfortable and coupled with the exhaustive schedule I kept, I went to sleep fairly quickly. About one or two o'clock in the morning, I went to the bathroom and Gina hadn't moved; she was basically in the same position she had been three hours earlier. Difficult as it may be to believe, I was far more aroused lying in a Greek hayfield between three nurses than I was with a naked woman fifteen feet away. Perhaps our disparity in ages was a factor, or possibly it was because the woman was the mother of a good friend—I simply don't know. Without lingering, I returned to the sofa and slept soundly to well past sun-up.

By the time I went to the bathroom in the morning, Gina had rolled onto her side facing the doorway and had covered the bottom half of her body with a sheet. However, she was still sleeping soundly. I went to the kitchen table to write letters home and even though it took me a while to write them, Gina remained in bed. I had the apartment key, so I left to mail the letters. It was after 10:00 a.m. when I returned and Gina was just getting up. She fixed me some toast and jelly, but unlike the night before, our conversation was strained and awkward. I sensed her nervousness and she sensed mine. I made some excuse about having to hurry along to get back to start school on time. She said she hated to see me go so quickly, yet never asked me to stay longer. The whole situation might have been much different, I'm sure, if Greg had been home.

Gina had no car, therefore it took me several city buses and more than two hours to get to the west edge of the city. During that time, I thought about what happened—or what didn't happen in that apartment. Why did she leave her bedroom door wide open? Did she try to seduce me, if not overtly, then covertly?

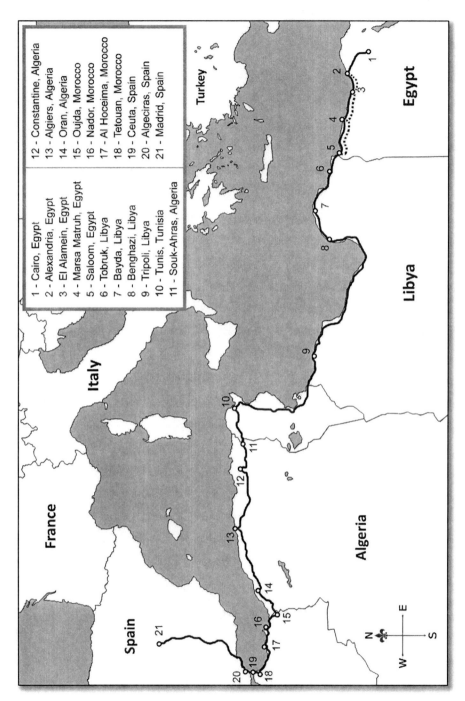

1 - Cairo, Egypt
2 - Alexandria, Egypt
3 - El Alamein, Egypt
4 - Marsa Matruh, Egypt
5 - Saloom, Egypt
6 - Tobruk, Libya
7 - Bayda, Libya
8 - Benghazi, Libya
9 - Tripoli, Libya
10 - Tunis, Tunisia
11 - Souk-Ahras, Algeria

12 - Constantine, Algeria
13 - Algiers, Algeria
14 - Oran, Algeria
15 - Oujda, Morocco
16 - Nador, Morocco
17 - Al Hoceima, Morocco
18 - Tetouan, Morocco
19 - Ceuta, Spain
20 - Algeciras, Spain
21 - Madrid, Spain

Cairo, Egypt to Madrid, Spain

Would I have gone with her if she invited me into her bedroom? Did she want to invite me, yet was afraid Greg or Sarah might find out? Did the abruptness under which we parted mean she didn't trust having a horny teenager in her house, or maybe she didn't trust herself? Nearly five decades later, those questions remain unanswered, but every time I see the movie *The Graduate* (where Anne Baxter seduces Dustin Hoffman—her daughter's boyfriend), I think of a strange night in Benghazi.

I didn't know what God's divine plan held for me, but I knew it wasn't to be a voyeur—particularly when the subject of the voyeurism was the mother of a good friend. Fifteen months later, as a soldier stationed at Fort Ord, California, I hitchhiked to northern California two or three times to visit Sarah and her new husband. I told her of spending the night in Benghazi with her mother, but I didn't mention anything about the details of the stay. Twenty years later, when Sarah visited me in Holcomb, the subject never came up. I haven't seen her since, but if she reads this story, she'll know.

It doesn't take a lot of mental effort to hitchhike, yet for all that day and for many that followed, images of that night in Benghazi stayed in my mind and it was tough to focus on anything else. Thoughts of the potential seduction even drowned out my memories of the polygamous school teacher and of getting back to college by early September. Only God knows how, if something significant actually happened that night, it might have affected my future personal relationships.

It was after 2:00 p.m. when I got a significant ride southward from Benghazi. I say "southward" because the Libyan Sea forms an inlet or bay off the Mediterranean Sea, and the Libyan coastline curves almost due south before turning west again. Later in the afternoon, while waiting for a ride at a busy country intersection, I found two piasters, the Libyan equivalent of about six cents. I also found a fourteen-inch pipe wrench. In early evening, I got picked in an Army truck as a convoy of Libyan Army soldiers slowly made their way westward. They stopped for the night on the outskirts of a small town. After walking into town for some crackers and Coke, I returned to the Army's bivouac site and slept on the back seat of an Army sedan.

When the soldiers woke up, we continued slowly on our westward march. We hadn't traveled an hour before they stopped and took a two-hour break for hot tea and watermelon. Apparently, they were ahead of schedule because they certainly weren't in any hurry to get anywhere—but I was. I left the convoy and caught a short ride into the next small town. I had no luck getting a quick ride from there, so while I waited, I tried to sell the pipe wrench I'd found the day before. Somehow, the police heard about my sales efforts and picked me up and took me to the local police station. They asked a few questions, filled out a report of some kind, and let me go. Naturally, they seized my pipe wrench. I threatened to take up the issue with the American Embassy once I reached Tripoli, but in my heart I knew I wouldn't do it and they probably did too.

I was stuck in the little town (sans pipe wrench) for more than four hours when the Army caravan caught up with me. Again, I got in with them and even though they moved slowly, they took me west more than 100 miles. I was grateful when they gave me twenty-five piasters (about seventy-five cents.) When I left them the second time, I caught a truck ride to a town 150 miles east of Tripoli. There, I splurged on a real beef steak for sixty cents, then walked to the nearest police station. The police gave me a mattress and that's where I spent the night.

The police knew someone going to Tripoli and they woke me up in time to catch a car ride with an Italian going all the way to the capital. Short of money for either taxis or buses, I hitchhiked through the city and past the shores of Tripoli in less than two hours. Now, nothing but desert stood between me and the Tunisian border. By 3:30 p.m., I made it to the Libyan checkout point. I was thrilled to make it across Libya, the size of Alaska and the seventeenth largest country in the world, in such a short time. Admittedly, spending only one night in Benghazi instead of three or four nights as I had originally planned had a lot to do with it.

My smug sense of self-accomplishment was short-lived, however, when I discovered I had another thirty miles of the Libyan portion of the Sahara to cross. Thirty miles was the distance between the Libyan checkout point and the Tunisian immigration office. If I didn't catch a ride, the thirty miles might as well have been three hundred miles. I waited and waited. More than four hours passed. The traffic was sparse, yet I had caught rides in light traffic before. What was the problem this time? I was tired, hungry, thirsty, and impatient. The latter was nothing new; I was always impatient. Near sundown, in exasperation, I threw a rock at a passing car, not to hit it, of course, but simply to vent my frustration. To my amazement, the car made a U-turn and swung around to pick me up. I thought he might hit me or something, but instead, he offered me a ride. He took me through the thirty miles of no-man's land in west Libya and more than 150 miles into Tunisia.

Tunisia and Wrecks in Algeria

The kind driver who picked me up at the Libyan checkpoint helped me through the immigration and customs office at the Tunisian border. Thankfully I finally found an Arabic country that didn't require a visa. I'm sure if I needed to return to Tripoli to get a visa, I would have snuck around the border guards and entered Tunisia illegally. On second thought, I might not have gone to that extreme, but I was truly grateful for the relaxed Tunisian requirements for American citizens.

After midnight the driver let me out. I had no Tunisian money, so I thought it best to continue toward Tunis, the nation's capital. A truck driver picked me up and said he was going to Tunis, but after no more than twenty miles, he pulled over beside the road. This time, the driver made no attempt toward funny business and I slept tiredly yet peacefully in the back of his truck.

The truck driver awoke before I did and drove all the way to Tunis while I slept heavily in the truck. I knew today would be busy and feeling refreshed with the extra sleep, I dashed straight for the American Embassy in Tunis. There, I informed them I was nearly destitute and asked if they could lend me some money. Their response was predictable—no. They did say, however, they could send me home and my family or I must pay back the State Department. I wasn't crazy about that option and told them I'd still like to make it to Spain by way of Algeria and Morocco. Pointedly, the embassy advised me to avoid Algeria because the government had just undergone a coup and changed leadership. Although the coup was generally peaceful, some isolated areas of unrest still lingered and it might be dangerous if I ended up in the wrong place at the wrong time. In addition, Algeria was another Arabic country that required American citizens to purchase visas before entering their country. Naturally, I needed to buy the visa at the Algerian Embassy, not the American Embassy.

I was getting really smart in my old age. For the third Friday in a row, I went to an Islamic embassy but this time, I *knew* they were closed for their weekly day of worship. I went anyway just hoping to get needed information, and I did. The visa cost was three dollars, but in addition, I needed four passport-size photos costing forty cents. For fifty cents, I found a hotel room near the Algerian Embassy to spend the night until I could obtain my visa in the morning. It was nice to have a bed and shower, but I paid a steep price. To get fifty cents, I had to sell the knife grandpa had given me for the trip.

It took two hours and my very last cent to get my visa at the Algerian Embassy. My very last cent—except for enough to mail two postcards home telling my folks and my girlfriend I spent my very last cent. True, I had a whole pocketful of coins from the many countries I had visited, but they couldn't be exchanged for anything at the bank. Banks exchange only paper money, not coins; therefore my coins were virtually worthless—good only as souvenirs. I was in downtown Tunis and wanted to make it to Madrid, a distance of more than 1,100 miles through Tunisia, Algeria, Morocco, and Spain. I had to cross the Strait of Gibraltar, too. Getting there would be a real challenge because—no ifs, ands, or buts about it—I finally ran out of money—completely out.

As the crude story goes, if you're up to your neck in excrement, be thankful it's not over your head. I found the analogy appropriate for my situation. I had no money to eat, but I wasn't hungry; I was sick. In the hotel room the night before, I spent more time on the toilet than I did in bed. I had come down with dysentery, the same thing Jenny picked up in Syria or Lebanon and carried with her to Egypt. She thought she got it from drinking bad water, but I seldom drank water and couldn't remember the last glass of water I consumed. I drank several glasses when I stayed with the Batarsehs in Bethlehem, but except for the water from the cricket-infested urn in that restaurant in Jordan, I hadn't had water for many days. Three weeks passed since I shared that coffee can of water with three other men, but that couldn't have affected me this many days afterward, could it?

The dictionary defines dysentery as a disease spread among humans through contaminated food or water. Once a person is infected, the infectious organism lives in the intestines until it's passed in the stool. As a gastrointestinal disorder, dysentery is characterized by inflammation of the intestines, chiefly the colon, and is almost always accompanied by diarrhea in which blood is present in loose, watery stools. Common bacterial causes of dysentery include some types of Escherichia coli (E coli) or other less common bacteria such as Salmonella. I don't know which bacteria it was, but I had the disease alright, and it could last for several days or a week. I always carried a roll of toilet paper in my suitcase, but as I left the hotel in Tunis, I borrowed another one from them in case one wasn't enough.

I made my way to the west edge of the city where at 10:30 a.m., I caught a ride in a mini-bus with eight other people. They dropped me off on the Tunisian side of the Tunisian-Algerian border. Despite all the paperwork and red tape I went through in Tunis to get my Algerian visa, once I got to the Algerian immigration point, they checked me over thoroughly, and I got through without incident. Listlessly, I walked less than a mile and then camped out by the roadside for two hours, waiting on my next ride. A short ride took me into the town of Souk-Ahras, Algeria, but I waited there for more than four hours. During the wait, a young boy came by and gave me two apples. I ate the apples, the first food I had eaten in two full days, and I began to feel much better.

For three or four weeks I thought about getting home before the fall semester began at the junior college. It was during this long, four-hour wait in Souk-Ahras that I made a clear and definitive decision. If at all possible, I would try to get home no later than the end of August. Certainly my decision was greatly influenced by being physically sick and out of money. Still, with this firm decision in mind, I was unsure how I would get back across the Atlantic. I procrastinated on that decision for a while; I needed to get to Spain first.

By nightfall, my next ride toward Spain put me in a small Algerian town where a taxi driver picked me up and took me more than seventy-five miles toward Constantine. The driver was heading that way and since he was alone, he gave me a ride for free just to keep him company. He stopped at another small village, even smaller than the one where he picked me up, and left me for the night. Everything in the town was closed and all the lights were off. So, in pitch dark, I walked a half-mile outside of town and found a harvested wheat field where I made a comfortable bed of straw and slept until morning.

More than three hours passed before I was picked up at my wheat-field hotel, but I got a long and fast ride with an English-speaking Algerian. We went straight through to Setif, completely bypassing the historic Algerian city of Constantine. The driver informed me the city is regarded as the capital of eastern Algeria and is the country's third largest city after Algiers and Oran. He added that Constantine is often referred to as the "City of Bridges" due to the numerous picturesque bridges connecting the mountains on which it is built. Alas, we clearly saw the mountains and a few of the bridges, but only from a distance. Along with the cities of Waterloo, Belgium and Naples, Italy, I wish I would have taken time to visit Constantine, Algeria.

When the driver dropped me off in Setif, he bought me a sandwich and Coke. I wasn't hungry because I still felt weak and nauseated, but I sure enjoyed the Coke. I know I was dehydrated and easily could have drunk three or four more. Without money, that wasn't an option. Lethargically, I ambled to the west side of town to catch my next ride.

On three or four occasions in small towns in the Middle East and North Africa, I rode in the back of two-wheeled carts pulled by either donkeys or horses. Most of the rides were short, generally a few blocks, but no more than a mile or so. The drivers seemed to be amused by hauling a red-headed kid with a suitcase and I was appreciative for the steps it saved me from walking.

As I made my way westward on the outskirts of Setif, a skinny Sorel horse pulled a two-wheeled cart going the same direction I was headed. The horse plodded along slightly faster than my walking speed. The cart was empty in back, but sitting in the elevated driver's seat were two old people, probably man and wife. When they passed by me, I snuck up behind the cart and without saying anything to them, I jumped butt-first with suitcase in hand onto the back of the cart. My suitcase and I didn't weigh much, but the force of my landing had the same effect as landing on one end of a teeter-totter. The two old people bounced in the air, the horse bolted for about fifteen yards, and my suitcase and I fell off the back of the cart. I'm sure my ill-conceived effort to save a few steps scared them half to death. The frightened couple turned around and cursed at me, which they had every right to do, and then sped away at a good-paced trot. I was happy neither of them had been thrown from the cart. Since no one was physically hurt, I found the incident amusing as I gathered up my clothes that fell from my opened suitcase. That fiasco was the shortest "ride" on my trip, and the last time I rode in a horse-drawn cart.

Embarrassed in front of the few people who witnessed my attempt at a cart ride, I hastily walked the rest of the way out of town. After a short ride of thirty-five miles, a large rich man driving a gold-colored Mercedes-Benz stopped for me. An adult man sat in the passenger seat and a young boy, probably the driver's son, sat in the back. I hopped in the back with the boy. We sped down the road at eighty to ninety miles an hour whenever possible. Not far ahead of us, a large herd of sheep, almost 200 head, congregated on the highway. The driver braked down to fifty or sixty miles an hour as quickly as he could, but too late. He hit two or three sheep, killed one, and the injured ones hobbled off the roadway. That type of accident was bound to happen sooner or later. (Little did I know the accident was a portend of things to come.) I saw hundreds of herds of sheep in every country since I left Italy. The desert and similar environs are without fences and are wide open ranges like those found in Wyoming and Montana. It's the shepherd's job to ensure the sheep don't get near the roadway. In this case, the shepherd, a young boy about twelve years old, failed miserably.

We all got out of the car and examined the damage. The driver's-side headlight was broken and part of the bumper and grill work was dented. The amount of damage wasn't terrible, but sufficient that both time and money would be needed for repairs. As soon as the driver saw the damage, he began a non-stop barrage of cursing and invoking the name of Allah in every other sentence. The driver yelled at the boy and the boy cried, but kept his distance eighty or a hundred yards away. Then, one of the funniest things I ever saw in my life occurred. The driver returned to his car, reached under the driver's seat, and pulled out a sixteen-inch butcher knife. With his two-hundred dollar trousers and Gucci loafers, he chased after the boy with the knife raised high above his head. The sight was reminiscent of the shower scene in the movie *Psycho* when Anthony Perkins attacks Janet Leigh. The man weighed well over 300 pounds if he weighed an ounce and was buoyed by a belly that would make a Macy's Santa Claus proud. The young shepherd wailed at the top of his lungs and ran twice as fast as the fat man chasing him. He needn't have worried; the fat man could never have caught him. The man ran only forty or fifty yards before he realized how useless his efforts were, and, covered in perspiration, he returned to the car and tucked away his knife. The temperature was too hot for even a person in good condition to run, let alone a fat man. He stopped running, but he didn't stop cursing.

The passenger, the boy in the car, and I endured the cursing for another five minutes until the driver stopped in a small town police station apparently to file an accident report and a complaint. The three of us waited outside in the shade of palm trees while the paperwork was completed. A side benefit to the delay was that I got to use the toilet in the police station; a real luxury since I was in the throes of dysentery. Two hours later when the driver finally came out, he had calmed down and we resumed our trek westward toward Algiers, the capital and largest city in Algeria situated on the Mediterranean Sea coast.

The afternoon was made up of several short rides until 4:00 p.m., when a car ride took me to Algiers. When I got out of the car, I asked the driver for some money to eat on. That was the first and only time on the trip I ever directly asked a stranger for money. Wasting no sympathy on me, the driver angrily and adamantly refused, saying he had just offered to buy me a sandwich two hours earlier. True, we had stopped for gas and sat down at the adjacent café where the driver had a sandwich and offered to buy me one as well. When he made the offer, my stomach felt like a churning volcano, so I passed on the sandwich but drank a glass of lemonade. The entire incident of asking a stranger for money left me so embarrassed and ashamed of myself that I never did it again.

Broke and thirsty (but not hungry) in the middle of Algiers, I found the nearest police station and asked to spend the night. They said no, but gave me a ride in a police car to a nearby Army facility. I suspect it was the local National Guard Armory or something similar to what we have in many towns in America. The person in charge of the armory also said no, and the police conveniently took me to a youth hostel. I had checked into staying in a youth hostel in London and once or twice in other cities, but had never stayed in one. Normally, youth hostels fill up by early afternoon and there's always a nominal charge. In this instance, there were empty beds and, since I was broke, I stayed for free. The shower and hot water were great, but having a toilet only a few feet away was fantastic!

Usually, youth hostels won't let their guests out until the beds are made, the floors are swept, and the entire place is cleaned and presentable for the next night's guests. An early riser like me had no chance to sneak out right after sun-up; the doors remained locked until 7:00 a.m. When the doors did open, it took about two hours to work my way to the west edge of Algiers. Feeling much better after the shower and a good night's sleep, I prepared to tackle the Algerian section of the Atlas Mountains that stood between me and the next major city in Algeria—Oran, some 225 miles west.

Actually, I had been traveling in the Atlas Mountains since I left Tunis. The Atlas Mountain range stretches across the northwestern part of Africa for about 1,600 miles through Tunisia, Algeria, and Morocco. If nothing else, the range provides a beautiful and cool respite from the monotony and intense heat of the Sahara. The highest parts of the range are found in Morocco, and the highest peak is Toubkal, with an elevation of 13,671 feet. Unbelievable as it seems, people can actually snow ski near Marrakesh. The mountains in Algeria are lower than those found in Morocco. Nonetheless, the Algerian countryside abounds with scenic mountain tops and valleys dotted with meadows, pastures, and enchanting mountain streams. As I left Algiers, the colorful rocks and mountain greenery were refreshing after coming through the barren, desolate, and dry Sahara in Egypt, Libya, and eastern Tunisia.

After less than an hour's wait just outside of Algiers, a car similar to a Volkswagen bug with two Algerian women inside stopped and offered me a ride. Neither spoke English well, but I was able to decipher they were going all the way to Oran, my next major destination. The driver was a doctor's wife and the other woman was single. The women were good friends, but were not related. I sat in the back seat behind the driver and my suitcase was on the floorboard behind the passenger. We hadn't gone far when we stopped at a pharmacy and the driver picked up some medicine which she took when she returned to the car. Less than an hour after that, we stopped again, and this time the women bought bread, tomatoes, cheese, and sodas for the three of us. I was thrilled. For some reason, I had a slight appetite and downed some bread and cheese with gusto—the first food of significance I had eaten in two or three days.

We stopped for a third time and the doctor's wife bought sixteen or eighteen bottles of warm beer. She grabbed one for herself and her friend, then offered one to me, but I declined. She then put the remaining loose, brown bottles in a small plastic laundry basket and set the basket between my feet. They each finished their first beer and I passed them another. After the beer stop, instead of slowing down, the driver increased her speed, at times reaching seventy or eighty miles an hour. I asked the single girl if I could drive a while, but she responded that her friend liked to drive.

In the Atlas Mountains somewhere between Boukadir and Relizane, Algeria, we hit a curve going too fast; perhaps seventy miles an hour. A car came from the other direction and to avoid a head-on collision, the doctor's wife swerved off the pavement. When she tried to correct the sudden change of direction, she lost control and the car flipped and rolled two and a half times. The car landed on its top on level ground about half-way between the pavement and a beautiful mountain stream some forty feet away. All three of us were thrown out of the vehicle. I went through the back windshield and landed on the pavement on my butt, back, elbows, and head. The single girl appeared to be totally uninjured and quickly ran over to her friend lying face-up on the dirt shoulder, thirty feet from the car.

I got up slowly but euphorically (because I was alive) and walked over to the driver. Her eyes were closed, she was making no sounds, and she was not breathing. I felt for a pulse near her wrist but didn't feel one. The single girl cried without restraint as she knelt by her friend, yet she offered no other assistance—nor did I. This was long before I knew about mouth-to-mouth resuscitation or pounding on someone's chest to jump-start the heart. Within the next five to ten minutes, an additional fifteen or twenty people stopped by and looked at the body. There was no doctor and no one offered help. She might have been unconscious, but all the witnesses, including me, thought the woman was dead. Perhaps she was; I never found out.

Glass had cut me fairly deeply on my lower left back and I had a four-inch gash just above my left elbow. Wearing jeans had saved my butt from serious scrapes, but the scrape on the back of my head bled for a few minutes before it stopped. I retrieved my suitcase and grabbed a shirt to dab the blood from my lower back and wrap around my elbow. I needed ten or twelve stitches above my elbow and half that many on my back. But when the blood stopped flowing, I thought no more about it except when picking glass out of both wounds for months afterward. (Eventually, I got all the glass out of my back. Almost five decades later, however, whenever I put my elbow on a table or counter top in a certain position, glass from that wreck will hit a nerve ending reminding me of a fateful day in Algeria nearly fifty years ago.)

Within thirty minutes, passersby had taken everything possible from inside and outside the car. The trunk was open and they took the spare tire and jack and other items that had fallen out, including the two suitcases belonging to the women. Although I didn't witness it, I'm certain both women's purses were stolen as well. Since the car was lying on its top, someone easily and quickly removed all four tires and wheels. Those not directly involved in the theft, stood and watched. If the car had landed upright, I'm convinced someone would have taken the entire engine and all its components. Remembering the thieves that stripped the car reminds me of an opening scene in the movie *Patton*, where Tunisian scavengers strip clothes and jewelry off dead American soldiers.

Although my shirt and jeans were a bloodied mess, I hadn't been hurt severely and I wasn't in pain. On that day and many that followed, I said many prayers of thanks to God that I lived through another fatal accident. At the moment though, I had something more important to think about. During the crash, the beer bottles had broken, spilling beer in the car and all over me. I smelled like a brewery, yet I hadn't had a drop to drink. I knew full-well it would be difficult to explain to the police if and when they arrived. The police never did show up as long as I was there, but a man and his wife picked up the lifeless body of the driver and took her and the single girl away—to a hospital, I presume. Once the women were gone and nothing was left to steal, the crowd dispersed and I caught a ride in a truck. I nursed my wounds and again thanked God for my good fortune.

Before I got into the truck, I found an Algerian map

and an Algerian coin, probably thrown out when the car rolled. The map was the first I used on the trip and I wasn't sure how much the coin was worth. After the truck dropped me off, two or three long waits and three or four short rides got me thirty-five miles east of Tlemcen, Algeria—a hundred miles short of the Moroccan border. It was well after dark when the last driver stopped at the edge of a village under a street light. He decided to sleep in the front seat and allowed me to take the back seat.

The car seat was comfortable, but my body was sore in many places. My injuries in the accident caused me to ache much more than after the customs guards beat me in Beirut. My mind whirled too as I thought back on the day's events. I reflected on a thought I had when I first got into the car with the two women. I hoped the ride would take me a lot farther than the fifteen-minute ride with the two women on the Ohio Turnpike. I allowed myself an ironic chuckle as I thought of the old cliché, "Be careful what you wish for." Before finally dozing off to sleep, I wrote in my diary, "This was the most unforgettable day on my whole trip."

Shortly after sun-up, the driver awoke and we made it the rest of the way into Tlemcen. The man gave me fifty cents and with that and the coin I found, I bought some food and savored every morsel. Physically, I was beginning to feel better, but mentally I was still shaken from the accident the previous day. Without a great deal of energy, I made it slowly to the west side of town, but got stuck there for more than three hours. There were no towns between Tlemcen and the Moroccan border, and apparently those making the trip didn't want a hitchhiker along for the journey. Eventually, a car driver picked me up and took me to the border. Before he did though, he stopped along the road, removed his driver's side headlight, and put some papers (or money) behind the light. The driver zipped right through the immigration line, but for some reason or another, it took me three times as long (an hour and a half) to check out of Algeria than it had taken to check in three days earlier. When I crossed the border from Algeria, I was both relieved and happy. I was relieved because it had been a struggle getting through the country particularly due to the accident, and I was happy because I had only one more African country to traverse—Morocco.

Sadness in Morocco and Joy in Spain

I waited over an hour for a ride from the Algerian-Moroccan border to the eastern Moroccan frontier town of Oujda. Using the map I had found the day before, I promptly took the wrong road out of town—so much for my map-reading skills. I backtracked about twenty miles and this time, I made a correct right turn and headed west. About an hour and a half before sundown, two men in a car picked me up and we zipped through the Atlas Mountains of eastern Morocco at a good speed.

We drove along a flat, level stretch of road in a broad, fertile valley with small mountains a few miles distant on both sides. Ahead of us, we saw five or six boys playing on the dirt shoulder right along the highway, almost close enough to touch the pavement. They were crouched in a circle as if they were playing a game of marbles or something similar. The boys saw us coming and stood up and moved away from the highway; all except one. Evidently disoriented, one young boy about eight or nine years old stepped onto the pavement directly in front of the car. The driver froze and although he honked his horn, he didn't hit the brakes and we hit the boy straight-on doing sixty-five miles an hour. The boy's body bounced on top the hood of the car, then fell off the driver's side onto the payment somersaulting and rolling until it stopped on the dirt shoulder on the opposite side of the road more than a hundred and fifty feet beyond impact.

The driver stopped immediately and we got out and ran back to the injured boy. His eyes were rolled back in his head, blood trickled from both his mouth and his eyes, and in a matter of seconds, his skin turned ashen gray. He exhaled one last time but never tried to speak and never breathed again. He had been killed instantly.

Besides the other boys, there were three or four adults nearby who witnessed the accident, including an old, gray-haired man. Unshaven for many days and wearing a long, white robe (typical shepherd dress in that part of the world), the man approached the boy's body. He began crying and wailing uncontrollably and then got on the ground and rolled over and over in the dirt for several minutes. Apparently, the boy was the old man's grandson or perhaps his son. Regardless, the boy's death and the old man's reaction was the saddest thing I ever saw. (Three years later, in Vietnam, I saw a number of dead American soldiers and many dead North Vietnamese and Viet Cong fighters. But I knew none of them and had seen none of them killed. Consequently, those deaths never affected me personally like the death of the young Moroccan boy.)

Unlike the accident the previous day in the remote Algerian mountains, there were a number of houses in this Moroccan valley. Someone called the police and they arrived within ten minutes. They questioned the driver, his other passenger, and me. It was an accident pure and simple, yet to this day, I believe the driver could have swerved into the other lane long before he reached the group of boys. The roadway was clear, it wasn't dark, and no car came from the other direction. Whether this accident in Morocco might have been avoided by swerving far into the left lane, God only knows. In America, truck drivers especially swerve wide, whenever possible, to avoid trouble on the roadside. Many car drivers do the same and after the Moroccan accident, I am one of them. In my heart, I suspect the accident could have been avoided.

During the ten minutes we waited on the police, I observed the driver. He had just killed a young boy with his car, yet he did not appear upset or shaken by the event. He made no attempt to speak, apologize, or console the old man in any way, and displayed no outward signs of remorse. Even after the police arrived, the driver seemed almost indifferent about the whole ordeal and seemed no more worried or distressed than if he had just received a parking ticket.

Accident or not, the police took the driver to the police station and released the other passenger and me at the parked car. I thought it might be a long while before the driver returned, so I grabbed my suitcase and walked westward a mile or more away from the people, the houses, and the scene of the accident. There, with nobody around, I cried. I cried as uncontrollably as the old man when he saw the dead boy on the ground. I had a flashback to a January night nine and a half years earlier. I had been asleep on the sofa in my maternal grandparent's house and woke up crying. No one said anything to me, but all of them were crying too, and I knew my brother had been killed in the car wreck. Later, my dad told us, and he stuck by his story until his dying day, that my brother Gary said to him "Daddy, I won't make it to Kentucky."

Alone in the Moroccan mountains, I thought of mom and dad and the unbearable pain and heartache they must have felt losing a child. I always felt closer to my father, but at that moment, I just wanted my mother to hold me. I was tired, hungry, thirsty, sick, and I hurt so terribly in the pit of my stomach that I wished for a magic wand to transport me the 6,000 miles to my mother's loving arms. With sincere regret, I never told my mother how very close to her I felt that day. It would have made her happy, I'm sure.

I experienced three wrecks in three days, two of them fatalities. I was mentally, emotionally, and psychologically shaken to the core, and remained that way for several days. The previous night, after the accident with the doctor's wife, I had written in my diary, "This was the most unforgettable day on my whole trip." I lied. The day we killed the young Moroccan boy was the most unforgettable day on my trip. Right or wrong, I lost a lot of faith that day and never again had the same spiritual perspective.

Startled from my sobering thoughts, a car stopped just before dark and we headed north and west to the town of Nador, Morocco. But I didn't want to go to Nador. Ships from almost all port cities in North Africa take passengers to Spain, but I wanted to continue west toward Rabat, Morocco, and cross into Spain at the Strait of Gibraltar. Nador was too far north and too far east. Everyone I asked in Nador thought I wanted to go to Spain by way of the port town of Melilla, Morocco, just a few miles north of Nador. I had a lot more trouble after I found a map then I did without one. I ended up in Nador unnecessarily, but all was not lost. I was able to scrounge three large tomatoes from one man and two Cokes from another and I ate for the first time that day.

After backtracking fifteen miles south of Nador to the intersection where I stood some four hours earlier, I was back on the right track. It was well after midnight and it had been an unforgettable and terribly exhausting day. After scribbling in my diary and drinking my second Coke (hot), I moved two hundred yards away from the street light and slept in a nearby field.

In the morning, I landed nothing but short rides west of Nador, but around noon, a bus driver took pity on me and gave me a free lift all the way to Al Hoceima on the Mediterranean Sea. When the bus stopped in Al Hoceima, the driver gave me some cookies and gum. I was thankful for the cookies and also thankful that I was finally on the right track westward. All I had to do was hug the coastline until I got to Ceuta, directly across the Strait of Gibraltar from Spain.

At the bus station I met a fellow hitchhiker, the first I had seen in many days. He hailed from Austria and was also going to Spain. The difference was, he had the money to get there; I didn't. Together, we walked to the west edge of the city and got a ride together with two men who were also going to Spain. A single car ride took the Austrian and me through the beautiful Al Hoceima National Park to the city of Tetouan, Morocco.

The two men in the car said the ferry to Spain wouldn't leave until 8:30 the following morning, so they intended to get a hotel room in Tetouan and drive up in the morning. The Austrian thought this was a good idea, so he joined them. Since I was broke and none of them offered to buy a room for me, I left them in Tetouan and hitchhiked northward out of town toward Ceuta. It's only a forty-minute taxi ride from Tetouan to the Mediterranean Sea port city of Ceuta, but, having no money, I had no choice but to hitchhike to the port.

On the map, Ceuta appears to be a port city in Morocco. In actuality, Ceuta is a peninsular Spanish enclave located on the north coast of Africa and shares a single western border with Morocco. The enclave and city by the same name lies at the junction of the Mediterranean Sea and the Atlantic Ocean and is separated from Spain by the Strait of Gibraltar. Its population consists chiefly of Christians (Catholics) and Moroccan, Arabic-speaking Muslims. Spanish is the official language. Geographically, Ceuta is similar to the Vatican, which is completely surrounded by the city of Rome.

I caught a northbound ride with a Moroccan farmer who turned off no more than two or three miles before reaching Ceuta. He dropped me off at 4:30 p.m., and there I stood and sat on my suitcase in the hot sun for more than four hours. Very few cars passed by. I realized that since the ferry departed the next morning, it might be best to just camp out there for the night. I would get up early, as usual, and just might catch a ride with the three men staying at the hotel in Tetouan.

There were no houses on my side of the road, but directly across from me was a beautiful, Spanish-style, two-story home with a mother-in-law house or servant's quarters in the back. The entire property was surrounded by wrought-iron fencing. The house had full-length verandas or porches facing the road at both levels of the house. All afternoon, two young girls ducked out of their upstairs rooms and looked at me for a few minutes then went back inside. Just before dark and before I started to bed down for the night, the father crossed the road and invited me into his home. The father and mother spoke only Spanish, but both girls, twelve and sixteen years old, spoke English well. The family fed me and gave me cold water to drink, and, with the young girls translating, we visited a while. The father offered me a mat and led me outside to the lower-level porch where I slept comfortably for the night.

The family that fed me and allowed me to sleep on their veranda took me to the Moroccan border with Ceuta. I had no problems with immigration or customs from either country and arrived at the port in plenty of time to catch the ferry to Spain. Since the father gave me the equivalent of four dollars in Moroccan money, I had more than enough to pay the $1.25 fare to cross the Strait of Gibraltar. When I exchanged the Moroccan money into Spanish pesetas, I lost almost a dollar in the exchange. Still, that left me almost two dollars. I wasn't rich, but it seemed like a lot of money at the time.

The crossing to the British colony of Gibraltar was uneventful except for the dominating sight of the Rock of Gibraltar. I can verify that the waters where the Atlantic Ocean and Mediterranean Sea meet are much smoother than those of the English Channel; at least they were on that day. As the ferry approached Gibraltar and I returned to the European continent, I took a minute to write in my diary, "Today is August 13th , but it isn't unlucky for me. I made it back to civilization!"

Around 10:00 a.m., we arrived at Gibraltar—the last British-owned colony on mainland Europe. The colony is an embodiment of English imperialism from centuries past, but now it's known mostly for its monkeys. The Rock of Gibraltar and the nearby area is home to Barbary macaques, the only wild monkeys in Europe. Originally from Africa, they can be ferocious, especially when people have food in their hands. The monkeys were the first wildlife I saw on my trip since seeing chamois or ibex at a long distance in the high Swiss Alps. Food was both precious and expensive for me, so I didn't eat in front of the macaques.

Five hours after landing, I barely made it outside the nearby Spanish port town of Algeciras. A car ride then took me to Malaga, the Miami Beach of southern Europe. Malaga enjoys warm winters with average daytime temperatures in the mid-sixties from December through February. But this was August and I wasn't there for the weather. I caught a truck ride to a major intersection where one road leads to Seville and the other leads to Granada. I took the Granada road and needed to travel almost due north for nearly 300 miles to reach Madrid.

After waiting only thirty minutes at the intersection, I experienced a stroke of good fortune as a truck driver stopped for me. He was going all the way to Madrid. I made myself comfortable in the back of the truck and we sped northward until well after dark. Even when the driver pulled over beside the road to rest, I was simply too tired and too comfortable to move. Contentedly, I slept the rest of the night in the back of a truck, knowing I would make it to Madrid the next day.

I was still sleeping when the truck started moving again and when I lifted the canvas flap, I saw a sign indicating we were less than a hundred miles from the capital. I was excited to make it to the big city, but something went wrong with the truck's engine and the driver pulled over for repairs. I hopped out of the truck, thanked the driver for the ride and the mobile hotel room, and walked to a café two blocks away. There, I spent the last of the previous day's four-dollar gift on a large sandwich and a Coke. In less than twenty minutes a young man about my age took me to Madrid and dropped me off directly in front of the main Madrid post office! An enormously impressive building for both its size and architecture, I ignored both and virtually sprinted to the general delivery window knowing full-well there had to be some letters from home. An elderly female clerk who looked long past retirement age curtly and rudely informed me there were no letters for me.

I left the post office dejected, particularly when I found out the American Express office was closed for the weekend. It was Saturday and I really wasn't sure if it were possible to get money from American Express anyway. I knew I couldn't get money from the American Embassy; they'd just send me home. That was always an option, of course, but I looked for alternatives. Spotting a nearby park bench, I sat down to think things through. I convinced myself there had to be letters for me in the post office. I wrote home frequently since Bethlehem and told everyone to forward letters to Madrid. I marched back into the post office, specifically asked for another clerk, and she gave me four letters—one from my dad, one from my paternal grandmother, one from a cousin Robin, and finally, one from my girlfriend Loretta.

With indescribable joy and suitcase in hand, I rushed to the nearest sidewalk café where I read each letter three times, crying through each of them. Except for a single letter from dad, these letters were the first contact from home I received for the entire summer. Although broke and 5,000 miles from home, I felt ten feet tall.

None of the letter writers knew I was out of money, but I was painfully aware of it, so I walked to the American Embassy to get help. The embassy didn't give me money, but they gave me the name of a pension hotel—the Sandia—and told me to check in there for the weekend. A pension hotel is a real hotel, similar in quality to a youth hostel when it comes to amenities. Still, staying at the Sandia kept me from sleeping on the streets until the paperwork was worked out. The embassy said they would begin working on my trip home on Monday morning, but their goal was to get me home as cheaply as possible, even if I had to wait three weeks for an empty seat on an airplane. They also stated they wouldn't rule out having me go back to America by ship.

The American Embassy in Madrid used pension hotels for people in situations like mine and the Sandia was far better than many hotels where I'd stayed in Middle Eastern and North African countries. My room had air conditioning and a private bathroom with a shower. I took advantage of the shower, re-read each letter four or five more times, and took a nap until evening. Finally over the dysentery, I felt famished. Although I had no money, I had an idea.

To me, Greek drachmas, of which I had several, and Spanish pesetas (dollars) look similar. They also weigh about the same. Perhaps in the dark, I might pass off the drachmas as pesetas and buy something to eat. I was especially hungry or thirsty for milk or milk products. I went to an ice cream parlor (*heladeria*, in Spanish) and ordered a single dip, vanilla ice cream cone. I took a quick bite out of the cone before I paid the young waitress. She caught me. She saw right away my coin was not a Spanish peseta. I pulled out a handful of Greek drachmas and showed them to her and, in broken Spanish, told her that's all I had. With disgust and contempt, she shooed me away.

I pulled the same stunt two or three more times until I had my fill of ice cream cones. Then, I bought a small package of potato chips and a young boy gave me Spanish change for my Greek drachmas. Thrilled to death with the exchange, I bought a large, cold glass of milk and a sweet roll. With a full stomach, I returned to my hotel and read Loretta's letter for the tenth time and wrote in my diary.

With the American Embassy, the American Express office, and the post office all closed on Sunday, I had few options. Consequently, I stayed in bed until 2:00 p.m.; unusual for me and the latest I slept since crossing the Atlantic on the *Tide*. When I finally got up, I stopped at a medium-priced restaurant a block away from the hotel and had a full meal of fettuccine alfredo. I sat at a table next to two businessmen—an American and an Englishman. During their after-dinner drinks, they invited me over for a nice, hour-long conversation. When they left, I left with them and didn't pay for my meal. The cost of my meal was just over a dollar and I told myself I'd return to the restaurant and pay them once I got some money.

With a full stomach, I walked around the beautiful

city of Madrid for an hour or two. Unlike most cities that boast a single style of architecture, Madrid had a combination of both Christian and Moorish architecture. The Moors defeated and invaded Spain (and southern France) in the eighth century and left Islamic religious buildings that still stand today. Architecture wasn't the only thing, however, that the Moors passed on to Spain. They also passed on a desire to conquer the world, albeit it was 700 to 800 years later when "militarized Catholicism" conquered much of the Western Hemisphere.

After I completed my Madrid walk-about, I returned to the Sandia and read the Gospel of John. Whether it was the wrecks in Africa or something else, I read the Bible with less enthusiasm and inspiration than I had in Bethlehem. Perhaps I knew I was a hypocrite by believing in the tenets of the good book while violating a basic commandment, "Thou shalt not steal." Disregarding my hypocrisy, I waited until dark and then tried my drachmas trick four more times. Twice I was angrily told to take a hike, but twice I got Spanish pesetas in exchange for my drachmas. When I returned to the hotel, I had Spanish coins in my pocket but I needed to come up with another plan—I was running out of drachmas.

It was after 10:30 a.m. on Monday when I made it to the American Embassy. In less than thirty minutes I decided to give up having the embassy send me home. Simply put, I would be going home at their convenience instead of mine, and it might take two, three, or four weeks. They advised me to contact TWA airlines. I walked to the TWA offices and asked them to call my dad and ask him to send enough money for airfare to New York. They wouldn't make the call, so I returned to the hotel and called him myself. I choked up with emotion while talking to him and told him how homesick I was and how anxious I was to return home. He promised to wire $400 to the TWA office in Madrid and he would meet me when I arrived in Kansas City.

I returned to the TWA office where I outlined our plan of attack. I hoped to borrow money from them until the airfare arrived, but they refused. On the way back to the hotel, I stopped at an expensive restaurant—the La Castafiore—and told them my story about waiting on money from home. In exchange for my passport, they let me eat all I wanted. They knew I wasn't going anywhere without my passport, and they weren't going to return it until I paid them in full. I returned to the hotel with a full stomach and as happy and joyous as I had ever been on my trip. All I had to do was to wait for the money from dad to be wired to TWA.

The next morning, I stopped at La Castafiore where I had established a charge account and had the best pancakes I had ever eaten. I left the restaurant in plenty of time to get to the TWA office exactly when the clerk told me to be there. I was absolutely ecstatic and my faith in God (or dad) was restored when I found out the money was there. He sent $400. (Later, I found out he used my 1959 Chevy Biscayne as collateral to get a loan from the local credit union.) That was the good news. The bad news was $400 would not get me from Madrid to Kansas City. I asked TWA to take the ticket fare from Madrid to

New York out of the $400 and give me the rest, but they wouldn't do it. They took out the airfare to New York alright ($325), but gave me only $20 change. I told them to wire the balance back to my dad. The TWA clerk said a flight was leaving for New York City in two or three hours, but I told her to book me on the next day's flight. She did.

With twenty dollars in my pocket, I returned to La Castafiore, paid my three-dollar tab, and retrieved my passport. I then went to the hotel and paid ten dollars for my four nights' stay and still had money left over. After a short nap, I went to the Museo del Prado or Prado Museum, the Spanish national art museum located in central Madrid. The museum features an excellent collection of 12th century to early 19th-century European art. Based on the Spanish Royal Collection, the museum houses the world's largest gallery of Classical paintings— oil paintings created by famous masters of art. And, as one might expect, the Prado has the single best collection of Spanish art anywhere. I stayed there well over two hours and thoroughly enjoyed the original paintings of El Greco, Goya, Velázquez, Van Dyke, Rembrandt, and Murillo. Goya's art attracted me the most since much of his painting showcases the sadness of human loss and a universality of feelings experienced by all people in times of sadness. For less than a dollar, I picked up a comprehensive guide to the museum's paintings to give to Mr. Ruggles when I returned home. I returned to the hotel knowing I was going back to the United States the following day.

Why in the hell I had carried a pair of dress pants and a sport jacket in a suitcase for 20,000 miles I have no clue, but I did. Today seemed like the best time to use them. After a long shower, I donned the monkey suit (without tie) and stepped out of the hotel to a bus stop and waited for the bus to take me to the airport. I got to the airport in plenty of time to make the 2:00 p.m. departure. I don't remember the size or nomenclature of the airplane, but it was my first plane ride and there were three things I remember distinctly. First, every seat was full, with about 180 passengers, I believe. Second, a Greek lady surely weighing more than 400 pounds, took two seats about four rows in front of me. The stewardesses had to rig a makeshift seatbelt to go around her stomach before the plane took off. Third, we stopped for just under an hour at the Portuguese capital of Lisbon. The fat lady and me and four or five others stayed on the plane; the others disembarked and went into the Lisbon terminal. Once back in the air, the entire flight from Lisbon to New York City took fewer than six hours. That was forty-five or fifty times faster than the boat from New York to France!

I crossed the Atlantic by ship and traversed the entire east-west length of Europe almost exclusively by land. I visited all the Mediterranean Sea coast countries in the Middle East (except Israel) and I navigated nearly the entire length of North Africa by land. In one sense, I was thankful for the experiences and the knowledge I gained, but remembering the accidents in North Africa, I was far more thankful just to be alive. I was ready to go home.

Last Stop, Canada

Well, that's stretching the truth a bit; I was not quite ready to go home.

When the plane landed at Kennedy International Airport in New York City, it took just over an hour to clear customs and immigration. I walked out of the terminal and caught a bus to Grand Central Station. From there, I took a subway to Yankee Stadium, undoubtedly the only one there in a sports jacket and carrying a hardbacked suitcase. Spending my remaining money on a ticket to the game plus a hotdog and Coke, I watched the Los Angeles Angels defeat Whitey Ford and the Yankees 7-3. When the game was over, I crossed the street and found a bowling alley where I sat down to decide what to do next.

As I sat in the bowling alley pondering my options, I thought back to five hours earlier when I first stepped off the airplane. A TWA agent tracked me down and said my dad had bought me a plane ticket to Wichita, Kansas and it would be leaving first thing in the morning. Then, I committed a most irresponsible act. I ignored the agent and later denied anyone ever touched base with me about a ticket to Wichita. Not only was I breaking the commandment about stealing, (the two-day binge of stealing Spanish ice cream cones), but I knew I would bear false witness to dad about the airplane ticket.

Another commandment somewhere in there says to honor thy father and thy mother. I'm sure I broke that one too. Accepting my status as a shameless sinner, I decided to hitchhike home by way of Albany, New York and Canada.

A few minutes before midnight, I got onto a busy northbound freeway and was picked up by a junk dealer in an old station wagon full of odds and ends and pieces of furniture. He was going to Albany, but about halfway there, his car blew a radiator hose and we pulled off to the side of the road. With no stores open in the middle of the night, he decided midnight requisition was his only alternative. He ambled off with some wrenches looking for a similar car from which he could steal a radiator hose. He left me to be car guard and I promptly went to sleep. Two hours later, he showed up with a radiator hose, put the "borrowed" hose on his car, and away we went to Albany. We arrived a little after sunrise and he left me off near a New York Turnpike interchange. I needed to travel the full east-west length of New York to get to Buffalo and into Canada.

Certainly, the fastest way across New York by land is the New York Turnpike. It's a short and quick 250 miles from Albany to Buffalo if you drive straight through. Admittedly, east-west travel in New York was much slower for those people a century and half earlier using the Erie Canal. The turnpike and canal roughly parallel one another the entire distance between the two cities. Canal or turnpike, I couldn't catch a decent ride all day, and it was after dark when I reached Buffalo, a destination normally reached in half a day.

In Buffalo, I took a right turn and headed north for Niagara Falls. Twenty miles north of Buffalo, a driver let me off near a late-night diner and I went inside to grab a bite. I filled up on two hamburgers, fries, and a Coke, but had no money to pay for them. A nice waitress my age paid for my meal from her tips and I got her address to pay her pack. (I did.) When I left the diner, darkness had fallen and the temperature turned cold. Having spent three weeks in the Sahara, anything below 85° seemed cold to me, and surely it was much colder than that. I found an open car parked near a gas station, climbed onto the back seat, and spent the night.

From the gas station, I had no trouble catching a ride to Niagara Falls. Unlike more than a dozen other national border crossings I had experienced, Canada allowed ordinary American citizens, particularly tourists, to enter their country without going through customs or immigration. However, when I got to the Canadian border, I had to scrounge a dime from a tourist to cross the bridge into Canada. Like millions before me and millions since, I was awestruck by the beauty and grandeur of Niagara Falls. I lingered on the bridge for several minutes just watching the unending cascade and the tiny boats below. I realized the beauty of this magnificent natural site was unlike anything I had seen since I left the Swiss Alps. A Friday in late August before most schools started in America was the height of vacation season, and it showed in the parking lots near the falls on the Canadian side. I must have seen cars from every state, including Kansas. But a man from Ontario, Canada picked me up and started me on my trek across Ontario province to Detroit.

Ontario province is Canada's most populous and the fourth-largest in land area. The province is also the home to Ottawa, the nation's capital, and Toronto, the nation's most populous city. On this trip, I saw neither of those cities. With nothing but short rides all morning long, I was slowly making my way westward through the province. When someone gave me a ride, and after we exchanged pleasantries, I told them the highlights of my trip and I that was thumbing my way back home to Kansas. Without blatantly asking anyone for money, most knew I hadn't a dime to my name. Drivers from my second and third rides in Canada gave me one dollar and two dollars, respectively. The two dollars from the second man was to buy dinner, he said. It's a good thing they gave me money because when I made it to Windsor, Ontario, I had to pay bus fare to cross over the Detroit River on the Ambassador Bridge. When I paid the driver with a Canadian dollar, he gave me change in American coins. Since I was going back to the states, I asked a fellow passenger to exchange the other two Canadian dollars I had with me. I believe the passenger short-changed me a little, but I was happy to have American money in my pocket, regardless of how little it was.

Once I stepped off the bus and touched ground in

Detroit, the international portion of my trip was complete. I had visited nineteen countries and been to or through each of their national capitals except Morocco and Canada. I felt a sense of accomplishment and a sense of fulfillment, yet at the same time, I considered myself the luckiest of the lucky. I was lucky to have escaped extensive detention in Lebanon and lucky to escape with my life from a wreck in Algeria. But I was back in the United States now and happy to be there. I would have been happier if the Detroit Tigers were in town.

Unfortunately, the Tigers were playing in Boston that weekend. (I saved a visit to Tiger Stadium and to the ghost of Ty Cobb until I moved to Ohio nearly twenty-four years later.) In less than two hours, I was outside Detroit and on my way to Chicago. In Kalamazoo, Michigan, a gentleman bought me a hamburger and Coke and offered me two dollars. I refused the money because he had bought me a meal and I still had nearly two dollars left the Canadians had given me earlier in the day.

By late afternoon, I was in Chicago and had high hopes of sneaking into a White Sox game at Comiskey Park. Through sheer good luck, I caught a ride on the correct southbound freeway going right by the field. The White Sox were out of town, but a long-haired British rock group—the Beatles—were giving a concert at Comiskey that night.

In my speed to get to the Holy Land and to return home, I missed many sites and events. Now, by a scant four hours, I missed the Beatles—the greatest rock group in the history of rock and roll. If truth be known, however, at that stage of my life I would rather have seen a major league baseball game. Besides, I was on my way home; I would not miss my next ride south toward St. Louis.

By midnight, I made it far south into Illinois and only sixty miles east of St. Louis. When the driver pulled off the highway to get gas, I got out at the truck stop and walked less than a half mile to a field where I lay down for the night. Unlike the poor day of hitchhiking when I left Albany, on this day I covered a great deal of the Midwest. I had gone from the state of New York twenty miles south of Niagara Falls though Canada, through Detroit, through Chicago, and almost to St. Louis. That would have been a good day's journey even if I were driving my own car. With the sound of eighteen-wheelers plowing through the night's stillness on the nearby interstate, I slept until sun-up the next morning.

Walking back into the truck stop, I paused long enough to drink a bottle of cold milk and eat some sugar-coated doughnuts. Interstate 70, one of America's major east-west routes, has thousands of long-distance truckers traveling on it every day. From the truck stop, I easily caught a westbound ride and thankfully, we bypassed north of downtown St. Louis and headed westward across Missouri to Kansas City. Three good rides got me to the east side of Kansas City. As we approached the city, I was wide awake and full of smug self-satisfaction when I spotted the exact interchange where my uncle had left me when my journey first started three months earlier.

With fondness, I remembered the young black college student who had given me my first ride as a hitchhiker.

I had every intention of stopping in Kansas City and spending the night at Aunt Billie's as I had done when my trip started. But when I reached Kansas City it was only 3:00 p.m., and in my judgment, mid-afternoon was far too early in the day to stop hitchhiking. To validate my thoughts, my next ride began on the east side of Kansas City and took me through and around the city's downtown area. By 4:15 p.m. I was west of Kansas City and had crossed the line into my home state. I almost completed the circle; I just needed another 375 miles to get to Holcomb.

Not being let off inside either St. Louis or Kansas City was a real godsend and saved me many hours and possibly a few dollars in bus fare. My fortune changed, however, once I crossed the Kansas border. It seemed like every ride I caught was going only to the next interchange. At 8:00 p.m. on a Saturday night, my luck ran out completely and I sat stranded on the south side of Topeka, Kansas. And I do mean stranded! For some reason, I found myself on a bypass around the city and the traffic was light. As dusk turned into nightfall, the amount of traffic dwindled to nothing. There were no houses, gas stations, or truck stops anywhere within sight, but I saw the lights of city buildings several miles to the north. On my trip, I waited for rides for two hours many times, three hours occasionally, and four hours two or three times. But outside Topeka, in my own home state, I waited six hours before I got a ride!

Impatient, frustrated, tired, and thirsty, I resorted to a trick I tried in North Africa. I threw a rock at the next car that came along—a black Volkswagen bug. With no traffic on the highway, the driver screeched to a halt, flipped a U-turn, and came back to pick me up. He was going west to Denver, Colorado and needed to get there as soon as possible. That meant driving through the night. We visited for fewer than fifteen minutes when he asked me to drive. We pulled over to switch places and I drove for the first time in three months. Except for one bathroom stop and one to get a Coke and coffee, I drove from just outside Topeka to Hays, Kansas. We arrived in Hays just after sun-up.

I needed to get to the south end of Hays to take the road south and southwest to Garden City and Holcomb. At that time, my grandfather's oldest brother Ab, and his wife Jesse, lived in Hays, but I thought it best not to call them before 6:00 a.m. on Sunday morning. (Ab was only 85 years old then; he lived to be 106, the oldest person in Kansas at the time of his death.) Years later, I got to know Hays very well. For over a year, I commuted from Holcomb to work on my master's degree at Fort Hays State University. Later, a favorite aunt and uncle moved there and I visited them regularly. On this day, however, carrying my suitcase, I walked the full twenty or thirty blocks from the interstate north of town to Highway 183 south of town. With no sleep the night before, I was dog-tired and vowed to take the first ride to come along.

That first ride was a milk truck. The truck did not

deliver milk to grocery and convenience stores, but a tank truck that stopped at dairy farms to pick up raw milk for processing. I wasn't crazy about making a bunch of stops at farms along the way, but he was going to Dodge City, Kansas. That wasn't Garden City or Holcomb, but it was close enough. I hopped in. We stopped at about a thousand dairy farms between Hays and Dodge City, or it seemed like that many. In spite of all the side trips on dirt roads and stops at dairy farms, I stayed with the truck and we arrived in Dodge a little before 1:00 p.m. The slow but methodical milk truck was my last ride as a hitchhiker on this trip. From a pay phone at a convenience store, I called dad and he drove the sixty miles from Holcomb to pick me up.

I was glad to see my dad and I'm sure he was glad to see me too. I'm guessing, however, he was severely torn between giving me a hug and beating my butt. Deep down, I'm sure he was upset because I failed to call him and let him know where I was since I landed in New York. He decided to give me a hug. Then, he told me how bad I looked because I hadn't cut my hair and not shaved the entire time I was gone. That wouldn't do; he wouldn't let my mother see me like that. Although we arrived in Garden City on a Sunday, dad called a barber who made a special trip to his shop on Sunday afternoon to cut my hair and give me a shave. Once presentable, dad took me home and I tearfully hugged my mother. She said, "Welcome home Kenny, we missed you."

Afterword

No one in my community ever took a trip like mine. When I returned, I received some short-term notoriety in the community and gave talks about my trip to a dozen civic groups and church gatherings. Although the thought crossed my mind, I did not enroll in one of many seminaries or religious-affiliated colleges in Kansas, but instead, signed up for my sophomore year at the local junior college. In the fall, I had difficulty concentrating on the tedious routine of college study and only stayed in school to fulfill my obligation toward a track scholarship in the spring. Everyday life, both in and out of school, seemed boring and anticlimactic. The boredom ended quickly, however, as less than two months after graduating from junior college, I became just another dog-faced GI training to fight in Vietnam.

Although I hitchhiked from Fort Ord, California to northern California and to Lake Tahoe, Nevada and twice to my home in Holcomb (all in military uniform), I never hitchhiked overseas again. The people I met, the experiences I gained, and the sites I witnessed on my nineteen-country trip—particularly the sites in the Holy Land, have stayed with me throughout my lifetime.

Later, as I studied history in college, it was always with a bent toward religion, especially in the courses I took through Brigham Young University when I returned from Vietnam. There, I was introduced to the religious atrocities of the Dark Ages and concluded they were dark solely because the church smothered free thinking and opposing viewpoints. In my view, the last 500 hundred years hasn't changed much. Close-minded thinking still permeates modern-day religious dogma. It may be the height of irony that even though I was exposed to the spirituality of the Holy Land at a very impressionable age, in my adult life, I have remained spiritually disentangled from standard church doctrine.

Instead, I turned to the temporal joys and wonders of our extraordinary planet. As evident by this story, frugality marked my first international trip. Arthur Frommer's early travel guide, *Europe on $5 a Day*, preceded my trip by eight years. Even though I never read his book, independently we both discovered low-budget ways to enjoy foreign travel. And without Frommer's guidance or influence, when airfares and ship fares are excluded, I too, traveled for $5 a day. Unlike Frommer, however, my trip included some real extravagances—attending numerous major league baseball games, enjoying carnival rides at the World's Fair and Coney Island, and visiting two of the world's most renowned museums—the Louvre and the Prado. Despite these differences and the fact we never met, we could have shared valuable information about thrift.

* * *

Even though family, job, business responsibilities, and

the shortage of money kept me from traveling as widely and frequently as I would have liked, I traveled when I could. By the middle of 2012, I had visited all fifty states and all seven continents. Thankfully, none of my subsequent travels was done on a shoe-string budget like the one in 1965. Although I did not pass on the concept of thrift to my children, I did, however, pass on the love of international travel. That's the legacy for which I am most proud. Now, all of my children and even some of my grandchildren travel abroad whenever time and finances allow.

In my view, the three most memorable sites in the world include the sheer size and volume of the Amazon River, the pristine terrain of Antarctica with its icebergs, glaciers, and millions of penguins, and the almost indescribable beauty and grandeur of the Swiss Alps.

Those three highlights aside, however, my most enjoyable trip was with my four daughters and niece to the Serengeti Plains in Kenya and Tanzania in 2007. That trip made me realize and appreciate the sheer joy of sharing travel experiences with those you love. Sharing exciting world-wide attractions simply makes traveling even more delightful and memorable.

Even though I have not achieved the standard set by Argentinean Emil Scotto who visited 212 countries and possessions, I have seen much of the world. Still, I retain a passionate desire to visit parts of the world and countries I have not yet seen. With good health and a little money, I hope to continue my travels until they lay me next to my parents on the hill north of Garden City.

In the meantime, I think Augustine of Hippo, Catholic saint and fourth century church philosopher said it best: "The world is a great book; he who never stirs from home reads only one page." Life is short. Read as many pages as you can.

Author's Notes

Mainland Europe, the Middle East, and Africa use kilometers to measure road distances and Celsius to measure temperatures. Americans are much more comfortable using miles instead of kilometers and Fahrenheit degrees instead of Celsius degrees. I am more comfortable as well; thus I used the American terms throughout.

In all but three countries—Belgium, Luxembourg, and Tunisia—I exchanged American dollars or traveler's checks for local currency. I avoided addressing the money exchanges or the monetary units of each country because the exchanges were not particularly germane to the story. The striking similarity between some denominations of Greek drachmas and some Spanish pesetas were the exception and became integral to the Madrid story.

Family names and the first names of the people I met on my travels including those of Bernie McPherson, Martin Evers, Garruth Ruggles, the Thorns, and the Batarsehs are real people. Other names have been changed to protect the person's identity.

CPSIA information can be obtained
at www.ICGtesting.com
Printed in the USA
FFOW04n1319170913
1802FF

9 781625 168306